CHAPTER 2

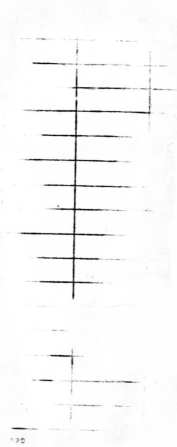

RIDING HIGH
Bicycling for Young People

ROSS R. OLNEY

RIDING HIGH
Bicycling for Young People

Lothrop, Lee & Shepard Books
New York

ACKNOWLEDGMENTS

The author would like to thank the following for photos, advice and technical information.

Dale Bennett, Matts Bike Shop
Pete Biro, Long Beach Grand Prix Association
Philip J. Burke, Bicycle Manufacturers Association of America
Todd Collart, expert cyclist
Ken Knott, Ventura Cyclery
Robert A. Loewer, Huffy Corporation
Jim McIlvain, Bell Helmets, Inc.
Scott H. Olney, photographer and darkroom technician
A. Virginia Phelan, League of American Wheelmen
Bob Russo, Ontario Motor Speedway
Patricia Shanley, model
   and especially Ken Bostrom of Schwinn Bicycle Company for his extra time and attention to this book.

Unless otherwise credited, all photos are by the author.

Copyright © 1981 by Ross R. Olney
Printed in the United States of America.
First Edition
1 2 3 4 5 6 7 8 9 10

Library of Congress Cataloging in Publication Data

Olney, Ross Robert, (date)
  Riding high.

  Bibliography: p.
  SUMMARY: Describes bicycle types and tips, safety, maintenance, bicycle sports, and "future bikes."
  1. Cycling—Juvenile literature. [1. Bicycles and bicycling] I. Title.
GV1043.O44   796.6   80-28566
ISBN 0-688-41979-8   ISBN 0-688-51979-2 (lib. bdg.)

TO MY FRIEND MICKEY SCHAFFER

CONTENTS

Bicycles use no fuel and leave no pollution.

1

BICYCLING REDISCOVERED

You feel great.

The sun is shining. The air is cool and crisp and clear and clean.

You are cycling northward from Morro Bay on Highway 1 through California's beautiful Big Sur region to Carmel and Monterey. Far behind is San Simeon, William Randolph Hearst's castle filled with treasures from all over the world. The way is more rugged now, but the scenery is magnificent and your mode of travel is the ideal way to see it.

Straight up from your side of the road rises an almost vertical wall of rock. Straight down from the other side drops the same wall hundreds of feet to the churning, foaming ocean.

You can hear the ocean far below, for you are not encased in an automobile. The ocean sound is not overwhelmed by the noise of an engine. You feel very close to nature here.

The wildflowers blend their fragrance with the cool wet smell of the ocean. You breathe deeply and your lungs respond; new energy flows to your body and arms and legs. The pedals move smoothly, with just enough resistance to keep the journey interesting.

It has been several minutes since the last automobile passed, so the air has been cleared by the constant breeze up the face of the cliff from the ocean. Drivers sometimes demand more than their share of the winding, two-lane road (you wonder if that is not more jealousy than need), but it is because of the unpleasant fumes it will leave in its wake that you find yourself dreading the next vehicle.

You take advantage of the moment and again deeply breathe the crisp air. Your legs pump rhythmically. You see the playful birds in the brushy outcroppings, the small animals scampering about now that the last automobile has gone. They do not fear you. They seem to welcome you, to be curious about you.

It is quiet. Only the birds, the chattering of the small animals, the swish of your chain in the gears and derailleur, the gentle hum of your tires on the road, softly intrude.

Highway 1 was hewn from the rock wall of the cliff along the western shore of California by thousands of Chinese and American laborers. With their bare hands and dynamite they cut the road, bridged the canyons, and built the highway many said could not be built. Now, today, you thank them as you roll on toward the village of Carmel, the boiling ocean far down on your left and the continent rising on your right. Cresting the road, you shift up again and coast evenly along.

The road seems to have been built for bicycling, but it is not the only ideal bike highway in America. Not by any means.

Have you ever cycled from the northwestern Ohio town of Lima over the back roads of the rolling Buckeye farmland to Indian Lake? Or ridden a bicycle through the Finger Lakes region in western New York State? Or pedaled through Central Park in Manhattan? Or ridden a bicycle around Gulfport, Biloxi, or Pascagoula in Mississippi, brushing aside the soft Spanish moss? Have you ever biked through Yosemite or Yellowstone, or the lake country of Indiana, or Michigan, or Minnesota, or Wisconsin?

Have you ever ridden a bike around the Indianapolis Speedway, hearing only the distant echo of the thunder that roars there on Memorial Day?

Or have you, in your own state, tried a bicycle along those roads you have traveled so often in a car? You have a treat coming if you move along slowly enough and quietly enough to enjoy

Bicycles are inexpensive, energy-efficient, and fun to ride.

the suddenly new sights and intriguing new aromas of your own home. You will arrive later, perhaps, but you will enjoy the journey more.

Bicycles, for years the favorite means of recreation, exercise, and transportation of an aware minority, have again become a prime mode of getting from here to there in a healthful way. It is no longer "backward" to ride a bicycle as a primary means of transportation. Young riders, especially, have discarded the artificial notions of the past to go with what they see to be the best.

The Perrier Company recently surveyed a national cross section of people of all ages, millions of them, to determine which physical activities of a sports nature are most enjoyed by Americans.

Walking, as you might imagine, was first as a physical activity. Swimming was a surprise second, since most people do not yet have a home swimming pool. The walkers numbered 34,500,000, the swimmers 27,000,000. Bowlers were third, numbering 21,000,000.

11

Kids know a good thing when they see it, and adults are catching on.

You might guess that tennis would be fourth, or golf, or roller skating, or even sailing. Or for that matter, what about running and jogging?

More than three dozen physical activities were discussed on the survey, including all of these and such far-down-the-list activities as rugby.

But number four? Millions of Americans of all ages—19,000,000, to be specific—named bicycling as their first choice. And more than one hundred million Americans regularly ride two-wheelers, though some of them list other physical activities as number one. They ride to school or to work, they ride for pleasure, they ride on vacations, they compete with other riders in races, hill climbs, motocross events and other two-wheel activities.

New enthusiasts every day are discovering the challenge of competition on a bicycle. From informal road races to high pressure events with Olympic class athletes, bike riders flock to participate. Younger riders across the country have been caught up in the BMX (bicycle motocross) challenge, a series of lightning-fast, rugged off-road races on specially made high-riser bikes.

Todd Collart, a well-known western cyclist and touring expert, says, "Cycling offers a unique recreational experience. Cycling offers physical and mental health, a way of putting you in touch with yourself. You can test yourself but you won't ruin yourself as you might when playing football or even jogging. If you have an hour to exercise, you can take a bike and go many miles and many different routes.

Bicycling offers a wide range of competitive events, from informal road races to high-pressure races with Olympic-class athletes.

Danny Ongais, a champion race-car driver, rides his high riser around the garages at Ontario Motor Speedway.

"If you believe in conservation, cycling is an efficient means of transportation."

Bicycles have become very important and will continue to grow in importance as energy conservation becomes more critical. In 1980, the federal government offered states up to four million dollars to promote bicycle use. Grants were made available for building bicycle paths or for any other project designed to enhance the safety and use of bicycles. Uncle Sam had finally come to realize the value of the fuel-efficient bicycle in an energy-conscious age.

What about the health claims? Runners claim that running is best. Swimmers say that swimming is best. Lacrosse players probably feel that lacrosse is best. The truth is, all of these sports are good exercise. The thing about bicycling is that you can get the benefit of healthful exercise and also get where you are going.

14

Younger riders love to test themselves during rugged BMX (bicycle motocross) events.

The late Dr. Paul Dudley White, a world-famous heart expert, said that bicycling was the best exercise of all. White, though by then elderly, regularly rode a bicycle as a means of exercise.

"There are four reasons I give for vigorous use of the leg muscles . . . not simply the arm muscles . . . and the first is physiological. We as bipeds need something to help us keep the blood circulating up from the lower part of our body.

"The leg muscles are very important," the eminent heart specialist continued in a Schwinn Bicycle Company motion picture called *Magic of the Bicycle.* "When they contract, they squeeze the veins (which have valves) and actually pump blood toward the heart. This allows the heart to receive more blood with which to supply the brain.

"This is physiological and, therefore, we have proof that it isn't simply the heart that is the only pump. The leg muscles are pumps

15

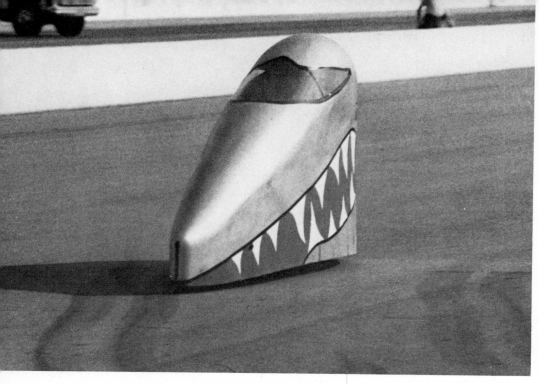

Other riders test themselves in other ways, often by racing on home-designed-and-built bikes such as this . . .

And this . . .

And this one for three riders.

and the diaphragm is a suction pump. So by keeping fit, we help the heart in its action.

"Psychologically, too, exercise such as cycling—it could be walking or swimming, but cycling is an especially favorable type of exercise—has a very good effect on the brain, on the mental state, and on the psyche. It's the best antidote . . . this kind of muscular exercise . . . for stress and mental fatigue. Instead of using tranquilizers, I advise muscular action . . . even to the point of fatigue, so that you won't need medicine to tranquilize you.

"We have a great problem today . . . and have had right along because we no longer use our legs properly . . . of being subject to thrombosis; that is, blood clotting in our leg veins. These blood clots can form and get established where there's too much stasis—sluggish circulation. This is a hazard to life because blood clots can go from our leg veins to our lungs and kill us.

17

This 1884 model is the Penny Farthing Roadster.

"The fourth reason, and perhaps the most important of all, is that there is clear evidence now that vigorous use of our muscles helps delay the onset of arteriosclerosis, which is the modern epidemic in this country today.

"These are the four reasons I give for vigorous use of the leg muscles such as that performed best, perhaps, on bicycles."

Health, fun, challenge, convenience, energy efficiency, pollution control—all good reasons for the growing popularity of bicycling today.

2
BICYCLE TYPES AND TIPS

Neither Dr. White nor any other doctor of the growing number who advocate bicycling is suggesting that you rush out and buy the first bike you see, then take off on a ten-mile ride. Bicycling is an uncomplicated activity, but there is some basic information you should consider first.

One man had to make a trip across town and his car was being used by his wife. He reluctantly decided to use his son's bicycle. He enjoyed the ride, and now he bicycles regularly. He was lucky to have been converted to full-time bicycling in spite of the fact that his son's bike did not "fit" him. The ride was probably not nearly as comfortable as it could have been. A carefully selected bicycle, chosen for the job it is to do, will be truly comfortable and easy to ride.

Few automobile drivers would try to make a little sports car tow a heavy vacation trailer, yet a sports car is fine for what it is designed to do. A heavy station wagon or sedan won't give you the joy of driving that a sports car will offer, but it can tow a trailer with ease and safety.

The same is true of bicycles. The fat-tired high riser is perfect for off-road competition. It is designed and built for this rugged use. But try riding it on a long-distance tour such as along Highway 1 in California. You'll be wiped out in a few miles. Your legs will be gone and you'll wish you'd never left Morro Bay.

Yet with a geared touring model bicycle you'll barely be warmed up as you skim along near Hearst Castle, and by the first rest

Americans rated bicycling their fourth most favorite physical-activity sport.

stop you'll be wondering why you always made the trip by car before.

The same bicycle, however, would not stand you well in a Grand Prime race with Olympic-class racers. For that you'll need a custom-built racing model costing up to four thousand dollars or even more.

The problem for a newcomer to the sport of bicycling is that there are hundreds of different models from dozens of manufacturers. To get the right bike, you have to consider use, type,

The man who rode his son's bicycle downtown was lucky, because he was also converted to cycling.

The fat-tired MX-type high riser bike is perfect for off-road competition.

The geared touring model bicycle is best for longer-distance pleasure riding.

To do well in a road race, you need road-racing bikes like these.

On an indoor track, racers go lightning-fast on bikes that have no brakes.

size, style, frame, saddle, gearing, tires, and many other factors.

But it isn't all that complicated. Basically, the types of bicycle boil down to three categories with a fourth, catch-all category.

BICYCLE TYPES

1. The first basic type of bicycle is the balloon-tired *high riser*. This bicycle is very popular with younger riders. You'll see hundreds of them in school bike racks and around the local ice-cream store.

The name "high riser" comes from the fact that the frame and wheels are small, so the seat and handlebars must be raised up to fit the rider. Sometimes the wheels are not even the same size, front and rear. Often the rear wheel has a knobby or heavily treaded tire for more traction. This is a durable, rugged bicycle that will stand up under the curb-hopping and off-road riding often demanded by younger riders.

This is the type of bicycle generally used for bicycle motocross (BMX) racing. A dirt racecourse with hills, dips, mudholes, sharp turns, and even drop-offs is used for BMX racing. Riders are protected with heavy clothing, pads, and helmets with goggles. Similar to motorcycle motocross racing, BMX is becoming more and more popular among younger riders who enjoy competition. Many cities are building courses for such racing.

High risers come equipped with fenders as a general rule, but many riders remove them to lighten the bike. Then they reinstall them for rainy seasons—otherwise, they get a line of water and mud up their back, thrown by the spinning rear wheel.

High risers usually have a "banana" type saddle, a long, slim, slightly curved seat. The seat might be covered with a glittering plastic. Up from the rear of the seat might project a curved roll bar, for whatever good such a so-called "sissy bar" might do.

Modern high risers might also be equipped with a selection of gears and brake levers. Or they might have a familiar one-gear and coaster-brake arrangement, where you pedal forward to go

The high riser (front) and the middleweight are two very popular styles of bikes.

and pedal backward to stop. If there are gears, gear shifting might be done by moving one or more levers, or by twisting the grip on the handlebar.

The short wheelbase and low center of gravity of high risers make them easy to maneuver and stable to ride, though many experts do not consider them as safe as the more standard types of bicycle. Equipped with knobby rear tires, they are excellent for off-road racing. With a wide, slick rear tire they can be used for drag racing. If you want to slide back on the banana seat and pump hard while lifting on the handlebars, you can do a "wheelie." Many riders can sustain a wheelie, with the front wheel well up off the ground, for great distances, though this is not a safe riding practice.

The high riser is a practical bike for paper routes because of the stability, and because the bags holding the papers can easily be slung over the high handlebar. It is a good bike for riding to school and on errands, and for just riding around town.

For more information on specially built BMX high risers and the companies that build them, read Chapter Five in this book.

2. Always popular is the *middleweight* bike. This is often the bike you go to after you have grown up on a high riser. This is the bike most teen-agers and adults buy for their first bike. The middleweight bike is one of the most practical of all bicycles. It comes with a standard diamond frame for boys and the drop-out frame for girls, and is a direct descendant of the early "Safety" bicycle. It even has the same general appearance as bikes from a century ago, with its balloon tires and standard frame.

The middleweight is designed for comfort and durability; with proper care and simple maintenance it should last for a lifetime of riding. The middleweight might be equipped with a gear system, lever-type brakes and high-pressure tires, though most still have balloon tires and standard single-speed coaster brakes.

The middleweight has a standard saddle, not a banana type, in different styles and sizes. It has fenders and normally has upright handlebars, called "all-rounders," and not the drop-type handlebars more common with higher-speed bikes (though some middleweights do have drop-type bars and all can be equipped with them if the rider prefers). With the all-rounder, the rider sits in an upright position, not leaning forward as with the drop-type bars.

The middleweight bicycle is light enough to be lively and quite maneuverable, yet solid enough to be durable. It is usually equipped with a chain guard to keep clothing from catching in the chain, and can be equipped with accessories such as speedometers, baskets, children's seats, and other equipment. It comes as a standard 26-inch-wheel model and in other sizes, depending upon the size of the rider.

For general pleasure riding, for riding to and from work, for errand running, for exercising, and for most other types of bicycle riding including some touring, the middleweight is the bike to buy.

3. Dedicated cyclists dream of owning a *lightweight*, truly a precision instrument that is expensive and delicate. Such a bicycle may weigh only 20 to 30 pounds, and it is as easy to ride as any bicycle built.

Lightweights come with standard saddles and all-rounder handlebars, but most have drop-type handlebars and narrow, un-padded saddles. They are often equipped with steel rattrap pedals with a cage for the toes, so that power is applied on both the downstroke and the upstroke.

The wheels on a lightweight are normally 26 or 25 inches, with high-pressure tires and inner tubes, though some racers prefer the sew-up tire, with no inner tube. These tires are glued to the rim and they are lighter and faster than regular clincher-type tires with tubes. But sew-ups are also rather delicate and much more difficult to repair in case of a puncture. They also require a special wheel rim.

Most lightweights are equipped with a derailleur gear system having five, ten, or fifteen speeds, and occasionally even twenty-five or thirty-six speeds. Most popular is the ten-speed system, offering a gear combination for most level and hill riding. There is also a popular three-speed lightweight in which the gear change is inside the rear hub rather than accomplished by a series of sprockets.

Lightweights for true aficionados have drop-type handlebars and are ridden in a forward-leaning position with the weight dis-tributed between the handlebars (40%) and the saddle (60%). Such bikes can make long-distance riding a pleasure, though they might not be quite solid enough for the heavy weight of supplies necessary for camping.

Probably the most popular bike type of all today is the lightweight, geared model.

4. Bicycles come in a variety of other types, sizes, and styles, with dozens of home-built models thrown in. There are bicycles-built-for-two (or more), called tandem bikes. There are tricycles (three-wheeled), unicycles (one-wheeled), and bicycles that fold up to fit into handy carrying cases. There are super-light, one-geared, brakeless bikes for velodrome racing on indoor tracks.

BASIC BICYCLE PARTS

There are a number of American bicycle manufacturers and several foreign builders of fine bikes (see the list at the end of this chapter). All of them generally call the basic parts by the same names. A bicycle is pretty much the same in any language.

THE FRAME

The heart of every bicycle is the frame, whether it is made of tubing better suited for plumbing or of fine metal specifically designed for bicycle frames and very expensive. The frame of a bike consists of the horizontal *top tube*, a *head tube* at the front, a *seat tube* or *seat mast* parallel to the head tube but under the seat, a diagonal *down tube* from the head tube to the *bottom bracket, chain stays* from the bottom bracket to the rear dropouts, and *seat stays* from the rear dropouts up to the seat tube, under the seat. This roughly diamond-shaped series of tubing is the single factor most determining the quality and the cost of the bicycle.

How many people do you suppose you could haul in the family automobile? Six? Seven? If you have a station wagon, you might even squeeze in nine or ten.

Consider the bicycle, one of the most efficient, hardworking vehicles imaginable. The "normal" load for a bike is about two hundred pounds. With accessories, a child's seat or any other addition, or even just a very heavy rider, this load can go up to three hundred pounds.

What this means is that a thirty-pound bicycle is expected to carry and support a possible three-hundred-pound load over all types of terrain. A three-hundred-pound load is about ten times the weight of the bicycle itself. On this very same scale, we should be able to ask the three-thousand-pound family automobile to carry thirty thousand pounds, or about one hundred and fifty people.

Yes, bikes are efficient and very strong. But they should also be comfortable and pleasant to ride. It is no fun huffing and puffing and being worn out by the time you get where you are going. The frame is the key.

There are three main measurements of a bicycle frame:

1. The length of the seat tube, from the center of the bottom bracket to the top of the tube.

2. The wheelbase, the measurement from the center of the front-fork dropouts to the center of the chain-stay dropouts.

3. The head angle, measured by the angle of the fork from horizontal.

The first measurement, the seat mast length, is critical for the proper "fit" of the bicycle to the rider. If a bike frame is too small, the rider will suffer early fatigue. This would be caused by the unnatural pedaling motion required.

The seat mast length is the number you will hear when the salesman is describing the size of the bike. If the number (the frame) is too large for the rider, the bike will be difficult to handle and unsafe to ride. Companies such as the Schwinn Bicycle Company manufacture bicycles with frame sizes running from 17 inches to 26 inches. (See the chart on page 62.)

The variations in the other measurements are not so great, but even a fraction of an inch or a degree or two of an angle can make a real difference in how a bike feels. A modern bicycle is pleasant to ride if it truly fits the rider. So why don't they just figure out the best possible lengths and angles and make all bicycles to these measurements?

The problem is, the changes in dimensions that make a bike more responsive, quicker to corner and handle, are just the opposite of the dimensions that make the bike more comfortable to ride. So the bike must meet an acceptable compromise, depending upon the use you plan to make of it.

The average middleweight bike you might use for normal riding should be easy and comfortable to ride with good shock-absorb-

saddle

top tube

caliper brake

seat tube

down tube

brake pad

frame

freewheel

seat stays

rear hub

chain

bottom bracket

pedal

chain stays

crank

derailleur

chain wheel

Basic bicycle parts.

Early cyclists learned that the larger the front wheel, the greater the speed in relation to pedal speed. So the Ordinary was invented.

ing qualities to make up for variances in the roadway. Such a bike would have a longer wheelbase (perhaps 42–43 inches), a head angle of about 70 degrees, and a fork rake (bend) of perhaps 2 inches. Such dimensions will allow the bike to absorb road shocks and give the rider a smooth, comfortable, stable ride, assuming the seat mast length is correct.

But this bike will not corner or handle as crisply as a racing bike, for example. Since the racer serves only one purpose (to go fast on a smooth track), it might have a wheelbase of only 38–39 inches and a head angle of 74 degrees, with a very short rake of only 1⅛ inches.

Of course the track bicycle will not be nearly as comfortable to ride.

Here's a tip to check the responsiveness of the frame on a better bicycle, if you can just ignore the groan from the owner or salesman. The test truly won't hurt the bike and will indicate whether or not the frame is "alive" or just a dead bunch of water pipes welded together.

Grab the bike by the front handlebar and tilt it away from you. Now put your foot on the bottom bracket and lightly push. The frame should flex slightly, then spring back when you remove the pressure. It should feel alive.

Try the same test on a cheap balloon-tired department store special and you'll feel the difference. One bike will feel springy and responsive; the other will feel solid, like the reliable transportation it could be—but little more.

THE FORK

The part of the bike that fits into the head tube of the frame and carries the front wheel is the fork. It is made of solid metal or tubular metal, just like the frame.

The "rake" of the fork is the amount of bend in it. The more forward the bend, the stronger the fork must be. But the more the bend, the more flexible and comfortable the fork will be. Generally, racers prefer a stiffer fork while pleasure riders like the springy, shock-absorbing feeling of a more flexible fork.

A tubular metal fork might not be quite as strong as a solid metal fork, but it will have more "give" and thus be more comfortable. Also, since the frame is the most expensive part of the bike, it will tend to be protected by a fork that gives in case of an accident. It is cheaper to replace a bent fork than a bent frame.

THE HEADSET

This is a series of nuts, washers, bearings, and races that holds the fork inside the frame head tube. These devices allow the fork to be turned inside the frame, which turns the front wheel. If the fork seems loose in relation to the frame, the headset probably needs adjustment (see Chapter Eight).

THE STEM

You might hear some cyclists call this part the "gooseneck" and that's OK too. It is the part that goes between the head tube and the handlebar. At one end is the clamp that holds the handlebar and at the other is the heart of the stem, the expander bolt. This long bolt has a head that can be turned to move a wedge nut at the lower end, clamping the stem to the fork inside the fork tube.

HANDLEBAR

Constructed of steel or aluminum alloy, handlebars come in a variety of shapes and sizes. Some bike shops will even bend one to fit you. The handlebar is mounted to the stem by a clamp that can be loosened for adjustment.

The two most popular shapes are the drop type, curving down and to the rear and generally taped (usually found on faster, lighter bikes), and the all-rounder. See Chapter Three for adjustment tips.

SADDLE

Saddle types and sizes vary almost as much as handlebars, with different types offered for different uses. The saddle is attached by a heavy wire frame and a bracket to the seat post, and may be moved up or down to make the final frame size adjustment for the individual rider. Saddles range from the zany "banana" types to thin, hard, springless cutaway models used by professional racers. You'll have to settle on the best type for you by trial and error, since that part of the human anatomy differs so much. Generally, though, you'll probably find the flared, padded, mattress type most comfortable (see Chapter Three for adjustment).

WHEELS AND TIRES

The wheel of a modern bicycle is made up of an axle, a hub, spokes, and a rim. If the wheel can be moved from side to side on its axle, there is a problem in the hub. If the wheel wobbles back and forth as it is turning, the problem is in the spokes (see Chapter Eight).

CHAIN

When Baron Drais invented the first bicycle back in 1816, it was little more than two wheels supporting a wooden crossbar. You sat on the crossbar and pushed forward with your feet on the ground. The *draisine*—also called a "dandy horse" or "hobbyhorse"—was crude, but it worked. A Scotsman named Macmillan improved on it about 1840 when he fitted cranks to the rear wheel and connected them by rods to foot pedals.

Then the pedals moved to the front wheel in 1862 and the "Velocipede" was born. Riders learned that the larger the front wheel, the greater the speed in relation to pedal speed. So the front wheel grew larger and larger until the "Ordinary" or "High Wheeler," also called a "Penny Farthing," was developed. The rider sat high up, almost directly over the huge front wheel, and falling became a serious matter.

Then along came an Englishman by the name of Starley. He developed a brand-new way of propelling a bicycle that has remained to this day. Starley put the cranks and pedals between the wheels and ran a chain to a sprocket on the rear wheel. The wheels could be made smaller and of nearly the same diameter,

Bicycles have come a long way from this boneshaker, popular back in 1863.

and thus the "Safety" bicycle was born. By 1886 the basic design of the Safety was perfected and, with many refinements, it is the bike we use today.

The chain was what made the difference. Your bicycle will operate with many problems, but if the chain fails, operation stops. The chain is the hardest-working and dirtiest part of a bicycle. Some modern chains have a master connecting link with an oversized chain plate that can be popped off and snapped back on so the chain can be removed for maintenance. Many ten-speed

An Englishman named Starley developed a brand-new way of pro-pelling a bicycle, by use of a chain, with the pedals between the wheels as on this 1889 Light Roadster.

chains do not have this link, so removal will require a simple chain tool for punching out and replacing rivets on whatever link you select. See Chapter Eight for chain maintenance tips.

BRAKES

It is easy, comfortable, and environmentally sound to ride bicycles. It improves your health and is less of a strain on your pocketbook. You can glide along over hill and dale, enjoying the method of travel you have chosen.

But there is another important factor to consider. If you can go, you must be able to stop. Baron Drais simply dragged his feet, once knocking down a neighbor's fence in the process. But he never got going fast enough to worry about it.

caliper brake

brake pad

On modern bikes you stop in a much safer and more dignified way, if everything is working. There are three popular types of brakes.

A *coaster brake* works on the rear wheel only and functions when you pedal in reverse. On most of the middle and lightweight bikes now, there will be a *caliper* brake system with a *center-pull* or a *side-pull* mechanism. This type of brake rubs a pair of brake pads on the rim of each wheel, one by the action of a cable pulling from the center of the caliper mechanism, the other by a pull on the side of the caliper mechanism.

Caliper brakes are activated when the rider squeezes a handle on the handlebar or on the top tube. They are efficient and safe if you work them correctly and see to their maintenance (see Chapter Eight).

GEAR CHANGERS

Don't make the mistake that some new bikers make. They think that if they buy a bike with three gears, they can go three times faster. A ten-speed bike should then go ten times faster.

Not true. The purpose of gears in a bike is to allow you to ride *easier*, not faster. The standard coaster-brake, balloon-tired safety bicycle has one gear combination. It falls in the middle of the combination gear models, as near as the manufacturer can get to a happy medium for level riding and hill climbing.

The trouble is, when you encounter a hill it is nice to have more power transferred from your legs to the rear driving wheel. Speed is not so important—you care more about getting uphill efficiently and with as little effort as possible. Three-speed and ten-speed (and even more) bikes allow you to shift to a lower gear combination (smaller pedal sprocket gear and/or larger rear wheel gear) so that the rear wheel moves slower, but with much more power, in relation to the pedals. You can continue the same rhythmic pace with your legs, but more power is developed at the rear wheel (at the cost of speed, of course).

Back on level ground, you can shift gears in the other direction (larger pedal sprocket gear and/or smaller rear wheel gear). Continuing the same pace with your legs, you are now transferring more rpm's (revolutions per minute) to the rear wheel but with less power, which you no longer need, so you go faster.

The trick among experienced riders is to set a pace that is comfortable for their legs, then choose the different gears as road conditions change. Unlike automobiles, bicycle gears are not designed to be used in consecutive order. You can shift from gear 1 (low) to gear 10 (high) on a ten-speed model without stopping in between. Or you can stop at any gear in between. The rider selects the gear according to the road conditions, a skill that quickly develops as you ride one of these precision bikes.

In general, moving the right-hand gear lever down will give a lower gear, for more power to the rear wheel. The same is true with the left-hand gear lever. But why do we need so many gear combinations?

The human body, like many other engines, works best within a narrow range. Moving too slowly or too fast requires a greater degree of energy. A constant pedal speed within your best range of efficiency will use your available store of energy most wisely. A constant speed will also help blood circulation in your legs, earlier mentioned as a tremendous health benefit according to Dr. Paul Dudley White.

Let's take a look at the ten gears on a ten-speed bicycle, the most popular model:

GEAR #1

This is the lowest, slowest gear with the least pedal pressure needed for forward motion. This one is best only for very steep grades.

GEAR #2

Another low gear. Good for longer grades that are not quite so steep.

GEAR #3

Best used as a "parking" gear. The equipment will not be damaged if gear levers are moved while the bike is standing still. Third gear is a "cross-position" where the chain goes from one side of the front sprocket to the farthest side of the rear gear set. It should be avoided when riding because of the extra friction, extra chain and sprocket wear, and greater energy required.

GEAR #4

For short hills and stiff head winds. An easy shift from seventh gear when moving slowly because the chain moves only from the larger front sprocket to the smaller one.

GEAR #5

Best for moderate head winds and tired legs. Good for a change of pace from seventh gear.

GEAR #6

An easy downshift from ninth gear for the small hills you wouldn't even notice in an automobile.

GEAR #7

Best for average conditions. With a rapid pedal rhythm, you can go on for the longest possible time before fatigue sets in.

GEAR #8

Use only for short periods. This is the other "cross position" where the chain goes from the other side of the front sprocket to the other side of the rear gear set. This is also a good gear for storing the bike since there is the least amount of cable strain.

GEAR #9

The tail-wind gear. Also for higher-speed trips that are short enough for fatigue not to be a real factor.

GEAR #10

Very tiring when used on the level for long periods. A high-speed gear, but your legs will tire in a hurry so that you probably will cover less distance.

Here's a valuable riding tip: Using the large front sprocket on a ten-speed bike (gears #3, 5, 7, 9, 10) most of the time will allow an easy downshift to lower gears on the small front sprocket (gears #1, 2, 4, 6, 8) for hills. The change, a quick move of one lever, should be made before it is needed, maintaining a light but steady pressure on the pedals during the shift.

The gear-changing mechanism is called a derailleur. Moving the lever pulls a cable and applies pressure to a plate that shoves the chain one way or the other. The chain then slips to a new sprocket. Ten speeds and higher have two levers: one to guide the chain on one of the two front sprockets, the other to guide the chain to the correct rear sprocket in the cluster of sprockets.

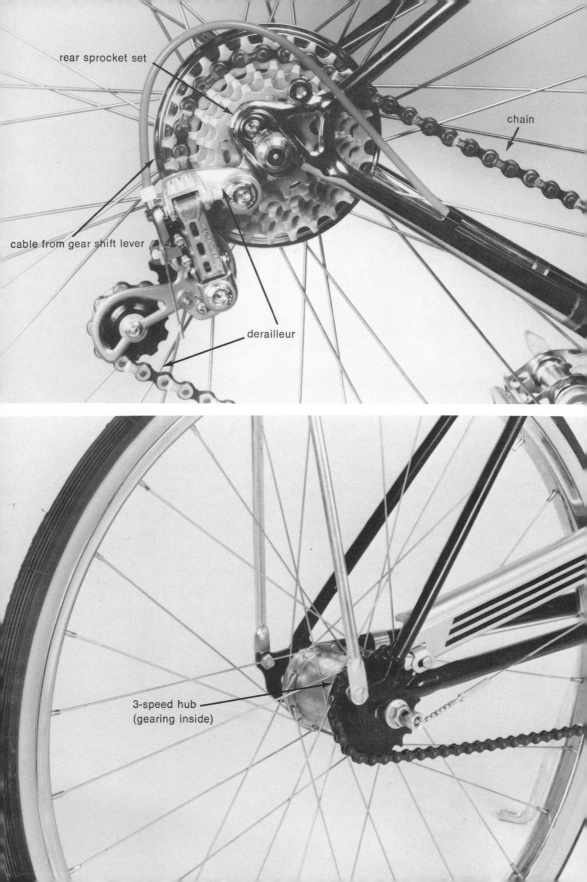

rear sprocket set

chain

cable from gear shift lever

derailleur

3-speed hub
(gearing inside)

A three-speed bike has the gear-changing mechanism inside the hub, but it is also activated by a lever or a twist of the handle grip.

FOR MORE INFORMATION

Here are some bicycle manufacturers you can contact for more information and catalogs.

Avocet, Inc.
P.O. Box 7615
Menlo Park, CA 94025

Ben Olken, Inc.
3 Bow Street
Cambridge, MA 02138

Bicyclesport Ltd.
175 King Street East
Toronto, Ontario M5A IJ4
    Canada

Campagnolo U.S.A., Inc.
P.O. Box 37426
Houston, TX 77036

Cycles Peugeot (USA), Inc.
18805 Laurel Park Road
Compton, CA 90220

Dawes M-Y Sport, Inc.
850 Sherman Avenue
Hamden, CT 06514

Dodsun Bicycle Manufacturers
No. 9 Nanking East Road
Sec. 3, Taipei, Taiwan, ROC

Fuji America
118 Bauer Drive
Oakland, NJ 07436

Hedstrom Company
Bedford, PA 15522

Huffy Corporation
P.O. Box 1204
Dayton, OH 45401

Klein Bicycle Corporation
1305 Maple Avenue
San Martin, CA 95046

Maruishi Cycle (America)
    Corporation
71 East Cherry Street
Rahway, NJ 07065

Panasonic Company
One Panasonic Way
Secaucus, NJ 07094

Royal Enfield
G. Joannou Cycle Company
151 Ludlow Avenue
Northvale, NJ 07647

Schwinn Bicycle Company
1856 North Kostner Avenue
Chicago, IL 60639

Sekai, Inc.
626 South Alaska Street
Seattle, WA 98108

Shogun Bicycles
Miami Bicycle Supply Company
407 S.W. 71st Avenue
Miami, FL 33144

Soma Sports, Inc.
Shofer's World of Wheels
8380 Baltimore-Washington Boulevard
Jessup, MD 20794

TI Raleigh (USA), Inc.
1170 Commonwealth Avenue
Boston, MA 02134

Toyoda America
5520 W. Touhy
Skokie, IL 60076

Vespa of America
355 Valley Drive
Brisbane, CA 94005

Worksman Cycles
95-15 100th Street
Ozone Park, NY 11416

Zebrakenko Bicycles
393 7th Avenue
New York, NY 10001

3
BASIC BICYCLING

On one commuter train serving New York City graffiti was never a problem. The cars didn't suffer the slogans and sayings usually found all over the subways. But cyclists have a pardonable enthusiasm for their sport. Such a bike lover, riding the train but apparently not by choice, wrote this announcement on the back of the seat in front:

BURN YOUR OWN FUEL—RIDE A BIKE!

Most of us could live without graffiti, but at least this short statement makes an excellent point. Bicycle are one of the best ways of all to travel, for ecological reasons as well as economical.

But to make bicycle riding a way of life, it is important to get a bike that fits you and to develop good riding habits early. The sooner you become a good cyclist, the sooner you'll be able to enjoy the adventures of the sport. As you learn the techniques, you will modify them to fit your own riding style, and eventually you will be as comfortable riding a bicycle as you are walking.

THE PROPER FIT

FRAME SIZE
The way to get the frame that fits you is to straddle the top tube of the bicycle with both feet flat on the ground. In this position you should be comfortably able to lift the front wheel

off the ground a couple of inches. Do this test in the shoes you will normally be wearing for riding.

SADDLE TILT

The saddle should be level or slightly tilted upward at the front. If the saddle tilts downward you will tend to slide forward and have to use unnecessary arm strength (energy) to keep in the saddle.

SADDLE POSITION

Draw an imaginary line or drop a plumb line from the top tube to the center of the bottom bracket. Then position the nose of the saddle an inch and a half to two inches behind this line.

SADDLE HEIGHT

Sit on the saddle and place one bare heel on the pedal with the crank arm down, parallel to the seat tube. In this position your leg should be completely straight. When you are riding properly, with the ball of your foot on the pedal, your leg will be slightly bent. But remember, at least two inches of both the seat post and handlebar stem must remain inside the frame and head tube.

One expert cyclist tests the saddle height by having the rider put both heels on the pedals (with somebody bracing the bike in an upright position). Then, while the pedals are being rotated backward, the pelvis should not rock. If it does, lower the saddle height a little and try again.

STEM LENGTH

Place your elbow at the nose of the saddle. Extend your arm and fingers forward. They should just touch the handlebar. If there is more than a half-inch overlap, or if you fail to reach the handlebar by more than a half inch, the stem should be replaced.

At least two inches of the seat post must remain inside the frame after adjustment of saddle height.

BICYCLE MANUFACTURERS ASSN. OF AMERICA

STEM HEIGHT

The stem should be level to or below the saddle. If the stem is above the saddle it is too high and you will be forced to sit too far upright, creating increased wind resistance.

HANDLEBARS

The top of the handlebar should be fairly level so that the hands can rest there comfortably without sliding forward toward the brake levers.

BRAKE LEVERS

These levers should be approximately parallel with the down tube, but slightly forward in a position that will allow you to brake easily and comfortably from either the top of the handlebar or from the dropped portion of the levers, if you have them.

The stem height must be correct and the handlebars must be properly positioned for comfortable riding.

SHIFT LEVERS

These levers can be mounted on the top tube, the down tube, the ends of the handlebars, or the stem. But shifters should allow the rider to work them easily without tempting him to take his eyes from the road ahead.

DERAILLEUR GEARING

As your experience on the bicycle increases, the details and technicalities of cycling will become more interesting to you. The *gear number* is a term commonly used by bikers to describe the ratio between the sprocket sizes controlling the distance a bicycle moves. A bike in a "75" gear will travel the same distance as a direct-drive model with a 75-inch diameter driving wheel (per pedal revolution). This is a carry-over from the days of the old high wheelers.

You can calculate the specific gear number by counting the number of teeth in the front sprocket being used, the rear sprocket being used, then applying the following formula:

$$\text{Gear number} = \text{rear wheel diameter in inches} \times \frac{\text{teeth in front sprocket}}{\text{teeth in rear sprocket}}$$

Here's an example:

$$27 \text{ inches} \times \frac{46 \text{ front}}{18 \text{ rear}} = 69 \text{ gear}$$

The gear number can be used to compute the inches traveled per pedal revolution. Here's the formula:

$$\text{Inches traveled} = \text{gear number} \times \text{pi} (3.14159)$$

Here's an example of this:

$$69 \times 3.14159 = 217 \text{ inches}$$

For most riding, a range of about 40 to 100 is right. If you normally ride in mountainous country, the lower end of the range might be 35 or even lower, depending on your own physical condition.

BICYCLING TECHNIQUES

STRAIGHT LINE RIDING

One of the most difficult things to do on a bicycle is to ride in a straight line. This is especially true when you are looking over your left shoulder to check on traffic coming from the rear. If you can learn to ride in a straight line no matter where you are looking, you will not be endangering yourself by swerving into the line of traffic. Drivers, seeing you ahead, will have confidence

One of the most difficult things to do on a bicycle is to ride in a straight line, as these experienced cyclists are doing.

that you will not be forcing them into another lane of traffic to avoid you in case of a swerve.

Practice until you can ride in a straight line even when you are riding very slowly and when you are looking away from your line of travel.

BRAKING UNDER NORMAL CONDITIONS

Always apply the back brake first and with a gradual, even pressure.

WET WEATHER BRAKING

Keep a particularly watchful eye ahead during wet riding to be sure you can see potential stops coming up. Then apply your brakes much sooner than you normally would, because your hands and the brakes are not as efficient in wet conditions. They will take more time than normal to slow you down.

LOOSE ROAD SURFACE BRAKING

Apply the rear brake first if it becomes necessary to stop or slow down while riding through gravel, sand, loose dirt, etc. Applying a heavy pressure on the front brake can cause the wheel to lock at a bad angle, resulting in a slide out of control.

EMERGENCY STOPS

In any emergency, get your weight low and to the rear of the bicycle, applying gradual but firm pressure to the brake levers. Do not "slam on" the brakes. That can cause the wheels to skid, resulting in a longer stopping distance and the possibility of falling.

BRAKE QUICK RELEASE

Many bicycles are equipped with a brake release lever that will allow for easy removal of a wheel from the frame. *Be certain to return the brake levers and cables to the original position after reinstalling the wheel, or you will have no brakes at all.*

ANKLING, TOE CLIPS, AND STRAPS

Ankling is a technique that helps to propel you more smoothly and efficiently without wobbling. To obtain a smooth and even flow of power from your legs to the pedals, bend the front of your foot downward toward the bottom of the pedal stroke and push the pedal in this manner *past* the bottom center. Then, on the upstroke, the front of the foot should be bent rapidly upward (dropping the heel), permitting pressure to be applied before the pedal reaches top center.

Ankling is the mark of an experienced cyclist and is especially helpful in hill climbing. The use of toe clips will help even more on the upstroke, since you can literally lift the pedal while the other pedal is on the downstroke.

Toe clips are also used to prevent foot slippage and to assist in proper foot placement on the pedals. Riding on the ball of the foot does more than increase efficiency—it is also more comfortable. Because the middle of your foot is a nerve center, riding with it on the pedals should be avoided.

GEAR SHIFTING

The basic rule for shifting gears is always to keep the pedals moving while shifting. Shifting the gears with the pedals stationary can damage the cables and derailleurs. But the pressure on the pedals should be gentle. Ease off just a little as you shift, but keep pedaling.

Research has shown that the "engine" in a human operates most efficiently in the pedal speed range of 60–90 revolutions per minute. The trick is to keep the pedals moving in this range, or toward the higher side of this range. Gearing should be selected to maintain this range. If you are idling in a gear that requires a great deal of effort, shift to a lower gear that will allow you to maintain the best gear and most efficient range. It is very important to maintain the best pedal rate on any hill you encounter, both to reduce fatigue and to permit earlier shifting when necessary. If you are aware that a hill is particularly steep, shift before

This young woman, like every other racer, uses toe clips on the pedals to help in ankling.

starting up so you won't get bogged down in too high a gear. That could cause you to make a rough, slow shift at the very last minute.

HAND POSITION

Hands should be positioned on top of the handlebar near the stem, midway between the stem and the brake levers, or on the brake lever housing.

When you are riding in traffic, keep your hands near the brake levers either from the top position or the dropped part of the handlebar. Sudden stops are often needed in traffic because cars pull out in front of you, traffic lights change quickly, a parked car's door suddenly opens, or for several other traffic reasons. You must be ready with the brakes.

If you are riding uphill, hold either the curved part of the

Research has shown that the "engine" in a human operates most efficiently in the pedal speed range of 60–90 rpms. These cyclists in the
1980 Los Angeles Grand Prime race use their gears to achieve this
efficiency.

handlebar or the brake housing itself. This makes better use of the muscle power in your arms, helping to "pull" you up the hill. You'll have to try this yourself before you get the real feel and understanding of it.

In a strong head wind, either hold the bottom part of the dropped bars or hold the brake lever housing and bend your arms. These positions will reduce your frontal area and your resistance to the wind.

HILL CLIMBING

Keep your pedal rate in the upper end of the efficient range by using the appropriate gear. As an alternative position, shift to a slightly higher gear than you would normally use while seated, then stand up to pedal. The main thing to remember in hill climbing is to conquer the hill gradually. Do not start too fast or you will tire rapidly. Hills can get to you both physically and mentally, so be cool and efficient.

DOWNHILL RIDING

Too much speed is the danger with downhill riding, so don't ride faster than your skill on the bicycle warrants. If you are riding down a steep hill, attempt to stop about halfway down just to be certain of your brakes and your ability to stop. Just like a semi-truck, a bicycle can suddenly be racing down a long, steep hill totally out of control. Once you have been in this situation, you won't want it to happen again.

On turns during downhill riding, keep your weight low and to the rear of the bicycle. Be sure to watch for gravel, oil, loose dirt, potholes and other objects in the road that could cause a spill. Be especially careful on blind curves, where you can't see far enough ahead. Maintain complete control of your cycle at all times, and especially while riding downhill.

CONDITIONING FOR BICYCLE RIDING

Any physical effort or activity, including bicycle riding, demands muscle motions that your body might not be accustomed to. In tennis, you might get blisters on your hands for the first few games. Some new players get blisters on their feet, and most get sore shoulders. But after some basic conditioning for tennis, the hands and feet get calloused and the shoulder muscles get toned for serving and hitting the ball. Many other sports make particular demands your muscles are not ready for.

In bicycling, it is not unusual to get sore in the seat and neck and arms during the first few rides. But a few basic conditioning rides will acquaint your body with the new demands being made on it, and it will respond. In addition, check over the following recommendations to ease any problems you might be facing.

UNCOMFORTABLE SADDLE

The best solution to getting sore in the seat, assuming you are riding regularly, is to use a good quality saddle made of plastic or leather. A leather saddle will "break in" to fit your own exact contours so that you will make contact with the saddle in the same places each time you ride. This will tend to toughen up these points and soon the problem will disappear. If you are riding distances on your bike, consider wearing riding shorts—but not so short that the insides of your legs rub unprotected against the edges of the saddle. The best types of shorts for bicycle riding have chamois lining to protect the skin.

STIFF NECK

Generally a stiff neck is due to craning the head to see while riding a bicycle with a dropped handlebar. Instead of craning so much to see ahead, lower your head and roll your eyes upward. You'll be able to see just as much but your neck won't get sore supporting the position of your head.

SORE BACK

If sore back muscles persist, change head positions more often, stop more frequently for rests, and do stretching exercises (see Chapter Seven) during those more frequent rest stops as well as before every ride.

FINGER NUMBNESS

A particular problem with new cyclists is the numbing of the fingers and hands, especially after longer periods of riding. This is apparently caused by continuous pressure on the nerves of the fingers, with a general lessening of circulation to these parts. The solution is easy. Change the position of your hands regularly during your ride and put a cushion between your hands and the handlebars. This can be done with extra, padded handlebar tape or by wearing riding gloves.

KNEE ACHES

If you are having knee problems, check to be sure your saddle position is not too low. Also, wear clothing that covers your knees when riding in cold weather.

THE FIRST RIDE

The lightweight bicycle, the model most riders eventually obtain and the best seller on the market today, is much more responsive and sensitive than the heavier bikes often ridden first. There is an art to moving from the middleweight to the lightweight. You will at first tend to overcontrol and even wobble around. Here are some tips to help you get used to a new lightweight:

1. Don't try to shift in the first block or so. Get a feel of the bike in whatever gear you are in when you start. Only when you can move your hand from the handlebar to the shifter and back a few times (without actually shifting the gear) while keeping

the bike on a straight path should you proceed to gear shifting. These lightweights are sensitive and will fool you at first.

2. Shift from top to bottom, front sprockets and rear, one gear at a time until you get the feel of things. Familiarize yourself with the positions of the levers and the gear combinations they represent.

3. There should be no noticeable change in the pedal rpm when the gears are shifted at the proper time (though in this initial practice on flat and level ground, there will be a change in speed of pedals). If, on varied terrain, you wait until a gear change is absolutely necessary before shifting, the change in pedal speed will destroy your rhythm and increase the fatigue factor.

4. Learn to use your gear combinations as they were built to be used. If you see a hill coming up, you don't have to shift to the lowest possible gear (unless you are riding a three-speed model). Choose the gear you need for the degree of incline.

4
BUYING A BIKE

The fact is, the more you pay for a bicycle, the less you get. That is, the cheapest bikes are usually the heaviest of the balloon-tired bombers while the most expensive bikes are lightweight and sleek in style. The very expensive ones are almost spartan.

But a bicycle is *you*. The world is changing. Sure, you can ride buses or subways, or drive your own gas guzzler to where you want to go, but buses are loud and polluting and subways are often dirty and crowded. Try to smell the flowers or truly enjoy the journey on these. No way. The family car is a growing anachronism. Gasoline prices are skyrocketing and so are initial costs, maintenance, and repairs.

You ride these vehicles without true consciousness. You get aboard and sit down and endure the journey to wherever you are going. You know the vehicle in which you are riding, and which you are supporting, is polluting the atmosphere. A bicycle, on the other hand, is a pollution *solution,* since it uses no fuel, emits no noxious fumes, and leaks no gasoline or oil.

The effect of riding a bicycle is immediate and direct and very personal, just the opposite of riding most other vehicles. You quietly control the bike, intimately and directly. You pedal with your legs and steer with your body and arms and it goes where you want it to go. You ask nothing from governments or oil companies or transit authorities. You make the decisions and you feel the surge of power from your body. You smell the fresh air and do not change it for the worse with your passing.

A bicycle is you, and that includes this unusual modification being enjoyed by a California boy.

In his book *Richard's Bicycle Book,* Richard Ballantine makes an excellent point. He says that moving a 150-pound person a few miles with a 5,000-pound vehicle is like using an atom bomb to kill a canary. Ballantine writes that the United States is unique in its ability to consume and waste, that the U.S. uses about sixty percent of the world's resources to benefit about seven percent of its population. Using a bicycle, according to Ballantine, is a first step to an "antidote to the horrors of U.S. of A. consumerism."

FRAME SIZES

Frames sizes for middleweight and lightweight bicycles range from about 17 to 26 inches for adult and young adult models. This distance is measured from the center of the bottom bracket

The effect of riding any bicycle, and especially a racing bicycle, is immediate and personal.

to the top of the seat tube (not including the seat post of the saddle). Generally speaking, frames are somewhat larger on boys' bicycles than on girls' bicycles because of the typically greater distance between crotch and foot of boys.

The first step toward buying a bicycle that is right for you is to get the correct frame size. Again speaking generally, the right frame size for you is a bicycle you can comfortably straddle with both feet on the ground. A girl interested in a girl's bike can use the same test on a boy's bike of the same size, then purchase the one with the girl's dropout frame (though many, many girls are now buying the so-called "boy's" frame or a frame with only a mild dropout, a relatively new design). If the bicycle doesn't fit you, it will never be as comfortable and easy to ride as it should be.

The following chart will give you a good idea of proper frame

If the bicycle fits you, as this bicycle fits racer Sue Novara, your leg will be slightly bent when the pedal is down.

size if you don't have a selection of bikes from which to choose. First, determine your leg length by measuring from your crotch to the floor while you are standing in your stocking feet. On all bicycles, the difference between the leg lengths in each frame size can be finally adjusted by moving the seat higher or lower.

FRAME SIZE	LEG LENGTH RANGE
17	26 to 30 inches
19	28 to 31 inches
20	29 to 32 inches
21	30 to 33 inches
22	31 to 34 inches
23	32 to 35 inches
24	33 to 36 inches
25	34 to 37 inches
26	35 to 38 inches

The high riser is fine for riding around the neigh-borhood or for BMX'ing, as shown here.

On high-riser models, the toes should touch the ground while the rider is straddling the seat. The handlebar grips must not be higher than the rider's shoulders when he or she is seated on the saddle.

A rule of thumb among cyclists for selecting proper frame size is to divide the rider's height in inches by three. If you are sixty-six inches tall (five feet, six inches), the right frame size will probably be 22 inches. Of course leg lengths vary, so try the frame-straddling test (feet flat on the ground) before buying.

It is very difficult to pick out one single model bicycle as a perfect buy. Different bikes are made to do different things. The high riser, though somewhat unsafe when compared to other bicycles, is fine for riding around the neighborhood, for BMX'ing when built for stress and with extra safety equipment, and for delivering newspapers.

The often mediocre department-store lightweight will also do the job of getting you around and the price will be lower, but the bike won't be built as solidly as one from a major manufacturer. Unless, of course, bikes with a major trade name are being sold by your local department store in the absence of a full-fledged bike shop.

The standard balloon-tired middleweight safety bicycle is also good for what it is built to do. This is a solid, reliable bicycle for general riding and riding on softer surfaces. Millions of them have been sold and millions more will be sold. This bike might come with a coaster brake and one gear, or it might have three gears or more in the rear hub.

Most popular today, for several reasons, is the lightweight ten-speed bicycle. For all-around use, this one might come closest since it can be used for errands or for getting to and from work and is also good for touring. Of the bicycles mentioned, this one is also the most expensive.

If you are buying a new bicycle, you are probably going to buy it from a bicycle outlet, a bike store, or at least a store with a large selection. You will have the advantage of a salesperson who knows bicycles. If you don't, move on to a store where the clerk knows what he is talking about.

You can discuss with the salesperson the uses you plan for the bike. You can try straddling several models to get the "feel" of them. You will have a selection of colors and accessories. The only thing you may not be permitted to do in some stores is to take the bike out and ride it. A shame, really, for this is the real test of any bicycle and whether or not it is for *you*.

If you are allowed a test ride, refer to instructions on page 69. If you can't test-ride the bicycle, ask the sales clerk and yourself the following questions once you have narrowed down to a particular bike:

You will probably be safest if you buy a bicycle built by a major manufacturer.

SCHWINN BICYCLE CO.

1. Does the frame seem solid and straight, without cracks or broken, sloppy, painted-over welds?

2. Are the seat and handlebars properly adjustable?

3. If so, can they be adjusted to fit you?

4. Are the wheels round and true?

5. Do they wobble from side to side on the hub?

6. Do they spin smoothly and freely, without noise?

7. Does each spoke have the same identical "twang" as you pluck them?

8. Are the pedals straight?

9. Do the brakes work positively and without noise?

10. Is the chain sprocket true and without wobble or looseness?

11. Does it spin freely, and without noise?

12. Does the derailleur work smoothly and without noise when you lift the bike off the ground and run through the gears?

13. Are the fenders firm, well braced, and not rubbing the wheels?

14. Is the seat correct for your planned use?

15. Are the frame lug welds smooth?

16. Will the weight of the valve stem pull the wheel around?

Here's a valuable tip when checking the frame: You can check the frame alignment of any bicycle, new or used, with a piece of string. Tie the string to one rear-axle dropout. Then run it up and around the headset and back to the dropout on the other side of the same wheel. The seat tube should be the same distance from the string on each side and at any point along the strings.

To protect the purchaser of a new bicycle, the Bicycle Manufacturers Association has a list of safety standards. The list is known as BMA/6, and all American manufacturers of bicycles try to follow these guidelines. They state that the bicycles made by member firms are built according to certain specifications, including strength of frame and forks. The width of the handlebars is covered, as well as the height of the saddle supports and other safety items.

A bicycle built according to these standards will probably have a sticker or some other identifying mark stating that fact. Such a bike should be of good quality.

BUYING A USED BIKE

A secondhand bicycle can be an excellent investment. Somebody else has taken the original loss, and if the bike has been cared for it can be almost as good as new.

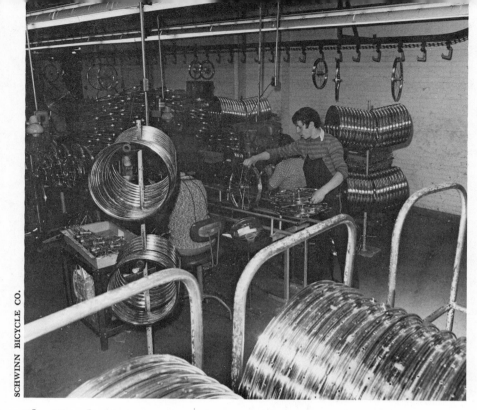

The Bicycle Manufacturers Association of America has a list of safety standards to which most American bikes are built. These wheels are being built by Schwinn to the standards.

You will lose the advantage of any guarantee and even the traditional thirty-day tune-up offered by many bike shops on a new bike, but the previous list of questions will work just as well for a used bike. If you learn about your bicycle, you can handle most of the matters that might come up with heavy riding of a bike that hasn't been ridden for a while (loosened spokes, gear changer drifting out of adjustment, lubrication, etc.).

Pay special attention to certain details of a secondhand bike before plunking the money down.

Check the paint very carefully. It will tell you a lot about how the bike was used or misused. Look at the paint and feel the paint, especially near the front joints of the frame. If you

BICYCLE MANUFACTURERS ASSN. OF AMERICA

Often your local police department will inspect a used bike for registration before you buy it.

find wrinkles or bulges, reject the bike as one that has suffered a head-on collision. The frame is probably weak and the bike may be unstable on the road.

Be careful if the bike has been repainted, for that might have been done to cover up such damage. At the same time, be logical. Parallel cracks in the original paint that are not quite hidden by new paint may not indicate serious damage. Be careful. Rate these matters along with the price and quality of the bicycle. A bicycle for a younger person, for example, might well have been repainted once or even several times, not to cover structural damage but just because the owner wanted a different color.

Many boys and girls make painting their bike an annual event every spring. They disassemble, clean, paint, lubricate, and re-assemble as much for the fun of it as for the nearly new bike that results.

So if you are buying such a bike, take that into consideration. On the other hand, if you are buying an expensive touring lightweight from a private owner, be very careful about matters such as paint. The owner of such a bicycle would probably have taken it to a bike store for painting, so no damage or flaws should show. In fact, it might even be difficult to tell whether the bike has been repainted.

The main frame tubes and wheels should be in perfect alignment, and the front wheel should be centered in the fork. Both wheels should spin freely and without noise. A wobble might indicate nothing more than a few loose spokes, or it could indicate a bent rim and the need for a new wheel. Remember, little wiggles can be worked out with careful use of a spoke wrench (if the spoke nipples aren't rusted solid, so check them too).

Inspect for dinged rims, a condition that will probably require a new wheel. On the other hand, rare is the used bike that doesn't need at least some repairs to bring it back up to the new owner's specifications.

Shake each wheel from side to side to be sure the bearings are solid and in good condition. Slack can mean trouble. While you are checking the bearings, move the cranks about to be sure there is no looseness in the hanger bearings. If you run into problems in this pedal bracket area, better reject the bicycle.

A TEST RIDE

You will be riding for pleasure after you buy the bike. Take this ride for business, before you buy it, to check out certain important areas.

1. Try the brakes, very gently at first and at low speed, just

to be sure you can stop once you get going. They should be solid and firm, with good stopping action and no grinding or squealing noises.

2. Run through the gears to be sure that each one engages solidly and without grind or squeal. The derailleur, if the bike has one, should move the chain with smoothness and a pleasingly soft "thunk."

On a derailleur-equipped bike, it is possible that you might have difficulty engaging the lowest or highest gear. This could be a matter of adjustment rather than mechanical fault, so don't reject the bike until you check this possibility.

3. The bike should track perfectly, with the rear wheel following exactly in the path of the front wheel when you are riding in a straight line. Make this test on level ground with no wind shifting the bike around. If the bike seems to drift to one side, ride back over the same surface to see whether the problem is with the bike or the road surface.

4. Balance should be easy and steering precise. You don't want a bike with sloppy handling. If the problem is a loose headset, it can mean an adjustment of the locknut or a replacement of bearings, a more expensive matter.

5. Tires are of relatively minor importance, except to indicate how much the bike has been ridden. Chances are, you will want to put new tires on the bike anyhow.

6. "No hands" riding, although not the safest procedure, is one of the best stability tests of all. Be careful, choose an open, flat, smooth area, and give it a try. You'll quickly feel the stability of the bike—or the lack of it.

7. Be skeptical of too good a bargain and don't buy a bike from a child unless a responsible adult is also involved in the sale. Don't be afraid to ask questions about the bike's background and previous owner. Ask for an owner's manual for that bike. Be sure the bike has the proper serial numbers and that they have not been altered or removed. If you knowingly buy a stolen bicycle, you are as guilty as the thief both morally and legally.

"No hands" riding, as Greg LeMond is doing here, is traditional for the winner of a race. It is also a fine test of stability for a bike you are considering buying.

COST

There are cyclists who feel that any bike under three hundred dollars is somehow "tainted." These longtime, experienced riders look for specific frame materials, expensive gear shifters, specialty tires and other exclusive parts. Perhaps this is true in any sport or activity where, as you grow and your expertise increases, you seek out the very best equipment.

These riders insist that when you move from a bicycle made for the masses to an elite model, the difference will astound you. The paint on the high-priced models, they say, is applied with love, and the bare metal parts are polished with great attention. The ride, because of the slimmed down and carefully tailored parts, is vastly improved. "Bikies" say that these vehicles are beautiful beyond their utilitarian function. They are mechanical works of art.

Buy as fine a bike as you can afford, a custom-built model if possible, but don't be afraid that if you buy a readily available,

"Bikies" consider their bicycles to be mechanical works of art.

mass-produced bicycle you will be getting anything but a fine machine. Modern bicycles are built on a production line, yes, but they are built with care for a lifetime of work and pleasure. Most experts agree that a modern production-line bicycle is at least as good as the super-expensive models of only a few years ago. Many are better, so fast has bicycle technology progressed.

You may not become a "bikey," a member of the cult. Most cyclists are not. They ride their bicycles for pleasure and utility, burning no fuel but their own. They get where they're going and enjoy the ride.

Be lighthearted but careful when you buy your bicycle. Listen to the clerk at the store or the current owner if the bike is second-hand, but remember that he may be a cultist himself. It will be

These riders have up into the thousands of dollars invested in their bikes, but you don't have to spend that much.

to his ego advantage and to his financial advantage to sell you a very expensive bicycle. He will be able to tell you why you should buy that model, and not the one from the row of less expensive but perfectly functional bikes nearby.

His words will make sense, for most of them will be true—but only from the point of view of an experienced, completely converted cyclist. Stick to your pocketbook range. Be not afraid. The bike from the row of bikes will do what you want it to do. The $149.95 model (a pretty fair chunk of money at that for a "reasonably priced" bike) will be fine, unless you can afford and are ready for the very expensive jobs.

The time might come when you will do as many other veterans

Major manufacturers generally guarantee their products for a much longer time than department stores do.

do. You will own two bikes, or three bikes, each one for a particular purpose. Then you will probably want the gleaming beauty, the geometric perfection, of a very high-priced model. Did you know you can pay up into the *thousands* of dollars for such a bicycle? Chances are, though, you will still ride your old-faithful model much of the time. The special bike will be used for special occasions, as it was designed to be used.

Meanwhile, attend a bike club meeting or a Sunday morning

tour of a local bicycle group. Non-members are almost always welcome, for that is where new members come from. Look over the bicycles in the racks outside, or as riders are preparing to leave. You'll see a wide array that will generally have but one thing in common. Every bicycle will be in good shape, well maintained by its owner. Chains will be clean and lubricated, gear changers in adjustment, paint and metal clean.

Beyond this there may be many makes, models, and price ranges. The club officers might be riding very expensive models, for normally they have been in the sport for some time and have grown into exclusive tastes. The broad range, though, will include standard models, secondhand models (somebody may have purchased the president's original bike), and even child seats, generators with lights, baskets, and other non-cultist accessories. You will be made welcome and treated with the respect every cyclist seems automatically to offer every other cyclist.

Whatever bike you finally buy, be sure to break it in. Check everything (bolts, braces, nuts, spokes, etc.) and then ride about fifty miles. Go back over the bike. Some bolts will have worked loose. That's why companies such as Schwinn insist that you bring the bike back in to the shop after thirty days to have it checked over. Very often something will have drifted slightly out of adjustment.

5
BICYCLE SPORTS

Bicycle sports are sweeping the country. You see more and more bicycles in the baggage sections of airplanes and trains as they are brought along by teams to out-of-town events. Or, of course, by passengers who want them along on vacations.

Here's a chuckle for you. Many countries have railroads that do not charge for hauling the bikes of passengers. In countries such as Mexico, Canada, Britain and many others, bikes are considered to be luggage and no extra charge is made. But not in the United States. The United States Government has increasingly urged citizens to consider bicycle riding as an alternate means of transportation, but U.S. Amtrak, a government corporation, continues to charge an extra fee for bicycles on its trains.

Even with sometimes paradoxical conditions such as this, bicycling is not something that is done to you, which is true of so many other things in life. Bicycling is something *you* do. In hundreds of local newspapers around the United States there are mentions of upcoming tours sponsored by local cycle clubs.

"Meet at the high school parking lot at 8:00 Sunday morning. The ride will be to [some nearby town or attraction]. A van will follow. Newcomers are welcome."

Give this a try after you have obtained your bicycle, or brought your current bike up to specifications. Basic touring is fun and the circumstances of these tours are usually non-demanding and certainly non-competitive. Nobody tries to beat anybody else to

These riders are ready for a road race, and almost all of them are Olympic-class racers.

the finish. Rather, the ride is for fun, for getting out into the fresh air and tuning your body while you enjoy nature.

Even if you have lived in your locality for years, as you ride your bicycle you'll see things you never noticed before.

In fact, here's an experiment you might try. Next time you leave your own neighborhood, pick out a single house or other non-prominent structure in town. Now visualize this structure standing all alone, without the surrounding structures and not necessarily in your town but perhaps out in the middle of a desert. Would you recognize it out of context?

Probably not, if you are a car driver or rider, even though you might have passed it hundreds of times.

Probably yes, if you are a cyclist, for cyclists tend to *see* their surroundings as they ride.

You'll be surprised, if you try the experiment, to find how often you will simply not recognize the things that are very close to you. Most of us do not have a chance to be good observers, moving as fast as we normally do through life.

You can even try this experiment with a local motel, business office, or other commercial outlet that you think would be very easy to recognize out of its own neighborhood. Chances are, you *still* wouldn't recognize it.

But the more you ride your bicycle around town, the more you will come to recognize things. You'll see things you never saw before. You'll notice trees, houses, parkways, lawns, flower beds and other beautiful (as well as the less attractive) areas in your own home town.

Today, communities are creating bike lanes in their roadways or pathways alongside the roads that are reserved especially for bicycles. This does not always mean that cars may not use these lanes, but bicycles are supposed to have the right-of-way.

You can help bicycling in your community by supporting bicycle lanes as well as using them. Put some pressure on your local representatives to have more bike lanes marked, with restrictions for cars.

BICYCLE TOURING

Real touring, instead of just riding around town, is attracting many cyclists. There is more to this than the aesthetic and physical rewards and the fact that you are conserving energy. Touring is fun. It is invigorating. Skimming along with a destination or goal in mind brings an inner joy.

Some people ride great distances on their bicycles. A few have ridden across the United States, or around the United States. A bicycle route running from coast to coast has been mapped for cyclists who dream of riding all the way across the country. Called

Bicycling is something you do, not something done to you, even with strange and mysterious bicycles built for speeds up to 50 or 60 miles per hour, as shown here before the start of a race at California's Ontario Motor Speedway.

the TransAmerica Bicycle Trail, it extends from Astoria, Oregon, to Williamsburg, Virginia. The route has been carefully selected by bicycle and transportation experts for scenic and historical interest, for varied views of rural America, and for roads where cyclists need compete as little as possible with motor vehicles.

To obtain maps of the route, write to:

> Bikecentennial
> P.O. Box 8308
> Missoula, MT 59807

Some cyclists carry along camping gear, while others prefer to stay in motels at night. Most cyclists carry little food on tours, preferring to eat in local restaurants along the way. This gives them an added chance to meet people and an excuse to stop in at least some of the charming or interesting small towns along their route. Touring cyclists plan stops at bicycle shops for equipment repair, wheel trueing, brake maintenance, and other necessary matters as they occur.

Here's a tip: rarely will a motel manager object if you bring your bicycle into the room at night. The best procedure is to go ahead and do it rather than asking for permission. Motel owners are quite accustomed to strange happenings, so sleeping with a bicycle will be mild by comparison. But do give them a break. Don't soil their carpets with your tires or scratch their walls with your bicycle. And use the service elevator where possible if you are on an upper floor.

Bike vacations have become very popular. One agency handling such tours booked nine thousand cyclists from the United States and seven other countries on tours totaling more than 280,000 miles. Another agency offers more than 120 different bicycle tours.

Information and a wide variety of touring supplies are available from companies involved in the sport. Write to them for more information.

Air Lift
2217 Roosevelt Avenue
Berkeley, CA 94703
  Mattresses

Banana Equipment
600 East Rogers Road
Longmont, CA 90501
  Touring clothing

The Bicycle Outfitter
973 Fremont Avenue
Los Altos, CA 94022
  Touring supplies

The Bike Bag
1650 Webster Street
Lakewood, CO 80215
  Touring bags

Bikecology Bike Shops
Box 1880
Santa Monica, CA 90406
  Touring equipment

Bike Warehouse
215 Main Street
New Middletown, OH 44442
  Touring equipment

Cannondale Corporation
35 Pulaski Street
Stamford, CT 06902
  Touring equipment

Eastern Mountain Sports
14203 Vose Farm Road
Peterborough, NH 03458
  Touring bags, clothing, accessories

Eclipse, Inc.
P.O. Box 7370M
Ann Arbor, MI 48107
  Touring bags, clothing, accessories

Frostline Kits
Frostline Circle
Denver, CO 80241
  Touring equipment in kit form

Kangaroo Baggs
39 West Main Street
Ventura, CA 93001
  Touring bags

Kirtland TourPak
Box 4059F
Boulder, CO 80306
  Touring bags

Moss Tent Works
Camden, ME 04843
  Tents

Pacific/Ascente
1766 North Helm
Fresno, CA 93727
  Rainwear

Pak Foam Products
181 Conant Street
Pawtucket, RI 02862
  Sleeping equipment

Redwood Cycling Apparel
1593 G Street
Arcata, CA 95521
  Touring clothing

Stereo Porta Pak
Sound Design
6430 Variel, #107
Woodland Hills, CA 91367
  Touring music devices

Ultra Light Touring Shop
Quarry Chapel at Wiggen
Gambier, OH 43022
  Jewelry, rearview mirrors, etc.

There are many more companies specializing in bicycle touring, and as interest in the sport grows, more new ones are created every week. A glance at a magazine such as *Bicycling* (33 East Minor Street, Emmaus, PA 18049) will reveal touring equipment manufacturers across the country. Most are happy to hear from potential tourers and will respond with catalogs and other information.

For information on full-fledged bicycle tours contact the following:

American Youth Hostels
National Campus
Delaplane, VA 22025

Cedok
3900 Linnean Avenue N.W.
Washington, DC 20008

Cycle Touring Club   Orbis
Cotterell House   2640 16th Street N.W.
69 Meadrow   Washington, DC 20009
Godalming, Surrey, GU7 3HS, England

These organizations will provide information on available bicycle tours, costs, accommodations, equipment needed, and other
details.

Not ready for a full-fledged, cross-country tour of several days
or weeks? Most bicycle clubs, and even a variety of informal
church, civic, and other groups are into "half-centuries," "centuries," or even "double centuries."

A "century" is a trip of one hundred miles.

You can test yourself against other cyclists, with nobody a loser
in these more demanding rides. They are being held in dozens and
hundreds of places across the United States. Typical of a century
ride, the most popular category, is the Ventura, California, "Sea
to Summit" ride. Cyclists leave the oceanside community of Ventura on a ride inland to Mount Piños, one hundred miles away.
Dozens of riders usually participate in this annual event and
they include cyclists of all ages and physical condition. The ride
includes long, flat stretches of highway and country roads pro-
gressing to uphill sections that demand more than average endurance.

For cyclists who choose to stop and rest overnight, there are
accommodations. Their ride then concludes the next morning. Most
riders, however, try to go the distance the first day.

Everybody has fun. The scenery, from the Pacific Ocean shores
to rugged mountain territory inland, is magnificent. The pace is
reasonable, with cyclists tending to break up into groups according to their own speed and fitness.

Half-centuries are fifty miles, and the rugged double-century
is two hundred miles. From your living room couch these distances might seem difficult, but on your trusty ten-speed with
your comrades around you, everyone helping everyone else, the

miles seem to melt away in laughter and fun. The more rugged parts are almost as enjoyable as you test yourself and your own endurance, knowing that if you stop and rest you'll have company.

For any trip longer than three hours, you might consider carrying the following equipment:

1. Bicycle pump
2. Lock
3. Tire patch kit
4. Small screwdriver
5. Small pliers
6. Brake blocks
7. Oilcan
8. Friction or duct tape
9. Small adjustable (crescent) wrench
10. Brake and derailleur cables
11. Cloth for wiping bike and hands
12. A small first-aid kit with basic bandages, etc., plus sunburn lotion and aspirin.

For longer trips you will need the above items plus the following:

1. Maps of your trip
2. A cycling cape or poncho in case of rain
3. Luggage carriers on your bike
4. A sleeping bag and ground cloth if you are going to camp out, and perhaps even a small, lightweight tent.

TIPS FOR TOURING

MAKING PLANS

1. Auto road maps and atlases show general areas and major places of interest, but not much else. Condensed topographical, geological, or bicycle road maps are far better. They are generally available through state and national park services, departments

of transportation, local bike clubs, and national groups like the League of American Wheelmen and the American Youth Hostels. These maps will tell you not only distances, but also topographical details (hills, etc.).

2. Mileage must be considered. At least one day of rest, however, should be planned for each week of touring. You may expect to ride an average of from thirty to seventy miles on your riding days, though adverse weather, poor roads, hills, or inexperienced companions can limit this daily mileage. Straining for too many miles will turn an enjoyable vacation into an endurance contest.

3. Transporting bikes as personal baggage is much easier than having them sent separately. Amtrak allows them "as is" (for a fee), but many airlines and bus companies insist on packaging. You should ask about this when checking schedules, and obtain a carton from your bike shop if necessary. Other options include traveling by private car or, more simply, starting out right from your own doorstep.

RIDING EQUIPMENT

1. If you are to be self-sufficient, your bicycle must be dependable and must carry everything you need. A ten-speed model with drop handlebars and forktip eyelets (for rack attachment) is best if you're familiar with it, but any properly fitted bike in good mechanical condition will do. If you have a choice, a wide gear range and high-pressure tires—85 to 90 psi (pounds per square inch)—are definite assets.

2. It is best to let your bicycle carry things for you, rather than strapping them to your back in a backpack. A rear rack is attached to the seat clamp or rear brake bridge. A pair of panniers (sometimes misnamed "saddlebags") straddle the rear wheel to hold camping gear. Because it is more accessible, a front bag carries the things you will use during the day and should be attached to a handlebar bag support. You will be able to carry everything,

even for wilderness camping, with these racks, bags, and your bicycle.

3. Some tools and accessories attach directly to the bicycle, including a tire pump, lights, a locking device (especially near "civilization") and water bottles, bell, and dog repellent. Tools such as a patch kit, screwdriver, and pliers should be carried in the front bag, for easy accessibility.

4. Other riding equipment in the front bag should include a rain cape, windbreaker, maps in a plastic pouch, first aid packet, sunglasses, and snacks. A towel or sweater fills space to stop any annoying rattles. If you don't carry it on your person, your wallet —with ID, phone numbers, and money (or better, traveler's checks)—should be kept in the front bag.

CAMPING EQUIPMENT

1. To save space and weight, take only as much as you will use on this trip. Half a bar of soap, a small tube of toothpaste, and small amounts of staple foods in plastic bags or containers will add to similar savings elsewhere. Packing soap in the mess kit and matches in the stove makes them easy to find and saves space for other things. In group travel, many items can be divided among the riders.

2. The panniers and rear rack hold everything not needed while you are riding, with cooking gear packed at the bottom of each side for the best weight distribution. A backpack stove with fuel should be included for the frequent times when a campfire is impractical. An aluminum mess kit, a can opener, waterproof matches (or lighter), scouring pads, and soap are packed with utensils, dishcloth, and staple foods like sugar, salt, and coffee. Vitamins, electrolyte tablets to help prevent dehydration, and health foods can be carried as diet supplements.

3. The clothing you take will depend on expected weather, trip length, laundry plans, personal preference, and activities planned, such as swimming and other sports. If you plan to haul along

two of everything, consider taking a pair of shorts and a pair of trousers as two trousers, for versatility. Clothes are rolled into plastic bags and placed in the panniers, or added to the bedroll if the panniers are full. A few extra plastic bags are good for carrying souvenirs and dirty clothes between launderings.

4. Sleeping bags are often graded for temperature comfort ranges. The more expensive bags are lighter and more compact, thus easier to carry along. You can also roll a small nylon tent with your mattress or ground pad, then tuck the roll into a water-proof bag and fasten it to the rear rack with elastic straps.

MISCELLANEOUS EQUIPMENT

1. The way you look will determine how well you are accepted by the "natives" along your route, and this is important when you ask for information, assistance or service. Besides soap and towel, it is important to carry a comb, toothbrush, and other personal care items. Avoid perfumed or scented toiletries and you'll reduce the need for insect repellents.

2. A small knapsack at the top of one pannier is handy for taking food from the store to your campsite. An extra water bottle, canteen, or folding water bag should also be considered, since you will need more water than on a regular bike hike. Some bicycle campers consider a pocketknife, a flashlight, and a ball of twine as necessities.

3. Reading, fishing, and bird-watching materials as well as a camera, games, and all other non-essential items are luxuries that you may take if you really want to. Remember, though, that small hills seem much larger under a load, and more weight increases the chance of a bicycle breakdown. A fully loaded bicycle can weigh *under sixty pounds*, a goal worth attempting.

WHAT TO EXPECT

1. After you are familiar with the camping gear, load it, then spend a full day riding as though you were already on tour. You will discover the different handling characteristics of a loaded

bike, perhaps causing you to reconsider taking some of the luxuries you planned.

2. Before riding, carefully check the bicycle for damage in transit (if it has been shipped to where you are beginning your tour). After seeing that brakes work and bags are securely fastened, shake the bike hard as a double check against loose gear. The first mile or so will give you a feel for load distribution and handling.

3. Start thinking about food and camping right after lunch, since country stores often close early and can be far apart. Enough food for dinner, breakfast, and a packed lunch is best purchased daily. Your maps should show parks, picnic areas, and camp-grounds, but inquiring locally will often lead you to even better places to camp.

4. Wherever you stay, be certain the area is left in better condition than when you found it. Then the next bicyclists will be just as welcome as you were. Before building a fire, check local regulations or with property owners.

MEMORIES

Even if photography isn't a hobby, you might consider packing a small flash camera in that last available space. Long after returning home you will enjoy photos from this trip. They will also help you in planning for your next bicycle vacation—which you will almost surely want to take.

BICYCLE MOTOCROSS (BMX) AND CYCLO-CROSS

The word "motocross," coined for motorcycle races, combines "motor" with "cross-country," and is defined as "a motorcycle race on a tight, closed course over natural terrain that includes steep hills, sharp turns, and often mud." An offshoot of the very popular motorcycle motocross events, bicycle motocross (BMX) has become one of the fastest-growing sports for younger riders in the nation. At first the regular high-riser type of bicycle was used,

BMX events are even held in big cities. This one is in downtown Los Angeles.

but now specially built motocross bikes are bought to take the rugged punishment of these skidding, sliding, jumping bicycle races.

Most races are less than thirty seconds long, but they consist of wheel-to-wheel and handlebar-to-handlebar duels between several riders who must negotiate tight turns on dirt or pavement, jumps over obstacles, and dashes up and down hills. The races are normally done on dirt, but in many cities there are also specially built courses on asphalt or pavement. Heat after quick heat, these races are run according to class and age of riders, both boys and girls. Champions are determined and in some cases money is paid. Certainly there are trophies for the winners.

In motocross there are also events for the highest jumps, the longest jumps, and the performance of tricks while the bike is in the air. The whole sport has become quite formalized, with recognized champions and a firm set of rules.

Bikes can cost up to $700, with the average cost being in the $200 to $400 range for a winning BMX bike. Such bikes are ruggedly built, with especially strong frames, tires, and wheels, and riders wear protective helmets, face shields, and leather suits similar to those motorcycle racers wear.

For further information on BMX and on Cyclo-Cross racing—bicycle racing on dirt field courses where the bicycle is often carried over hazards—contact the following manufacturers of BMX equipment:

American Cycle Systems
1449 Industrial Park Street
Covina, CA 91722

Chain Bike Corporation
Rockaway Beach
New York, NY 11693

Huffy Corporation
P.O. Box 1204
Dayton, OH 45401

Schwinn Bicycle Company
1856 North Kostner Avenue
Chicago, IL 60639

Skyway Recreation Products
4451 Caterpillar Road
Redding, CA 96001

TI Raleigh (USA), Inc.
1170 Commonwealth Avenue
Boston, MA 02134

Webco
218 Main Street
Venice, CA 90291

The national association covering bicycle motocross will also provide information on this rapidly growing sport for younger riders:

National Bicycle Motocross Association
P.O. Box L
Newhall, CA 91322

BICYCLE RACING

Cyclists streak around board tracks called "velodromes" (from "velocipede") at speeds up to fifty miles per hour. Clamped to their bikes by footstraps, they fight the centrifugal force that doubles their weight on every banked turn. Their heads and shoulders are pushed downward as they race their bicycles, extremely lightweight (fifteen-pound) models with no brakes and a single, high-speed gear.

On the turns, "catchers" are stationed to jerk fallen riders off the track so that following riders won't simply pile up. Remember, the feet of the racers are strapped to the pedals so they can't just get up and run after a crash. This is an exciting, dangerous form of cycling. Riders have been injured and even killed racing bicycles.

Indoor track racing is an American invention that packed the grandstands in the twenties and thirties. The rage spread to Europe where, even today, velodrome racing is still called "L'Américain."

Racers from other types of bicycle racing complain that velodrome racing is more like drag racing. There is no time to plan ahead or to recoup from the slightest mistake. Famous road racers, for example, have tried a few laps of a track and quit with shaking hands, so demanding is this type of bicycle racing.

Unfortunately, spectator awareness of this exciting sport is at a low level. From the old days when thousands jammed the tracksides to watch, the crowd has dwindled down to a few hundred avid fans at major races.

This may be changing, however. The Friday-night action at the velodrome in Trexlertown, Pennsylvania, pulls as many as five thousand spectators. And Madison Square Garden, in New York

These two riders are preparing for a velodrome race on a board track.

City, is planning three-day bicycle races in ten participating cities in the spring and summer, with the finals to be held at the Garden in the fall. Speaking of the excitement of these races and the crowds they will attract, the promoter said, "It'll be about two notches below 'Rollerball'."

At a recent race in Denver sponsored by the International Cycling Classic, a group that brings its own portable track to the race site, the spectators were screaming. The speed, the color, and the skill of the riders had captivated them.

"They're just like the good ol' boys ascreamin' round the Daytona Speedway," shouted one fan, "but here you can see the engines aworkin'. Look at those legs *go!*"

Track racing involves a variety of grueling, demanding, and even zany events. In the 1920's a popular form of bicycle racing was "six-day races." This form of bicycle racing is still very popular around the world. Two-person teams compete against each other for six long days of racing. While one team member is on the track, the other is resting. Spectators come and go during these events.

Short sprint races are popular. Record attempts on a track are popular. *Madisons*, named after the fact that they originated in Madison Square Garden in New York, are the most popular in this country. These are high-speed races in which partners keep alternating for one lap each.

There are events like the zany "Devil Take the Hindmost" that have grown rapidly as crowd-pleasing attractions. The idea of this race is simple. The field goes for three laps. If you are in last place at the end of the third lap, you are ordered out of the race. Then the pack goes for three more laps. Again, the last cyclist is out. This goes on until only two cyclists remain. The last three laps are a mad, wild dash for the finish line between the two.

Riders such as Belgian superstar Willy Debosscher, a professional bicycle racer, have a habit of *purposely* being in last place until the final quarter lap of each heat. Debosscher constantly brings the crowd to its feet as he frantically pedals the last few feet to edge out the next rider, all the time pointing out this rider to the judges alongside the track. He does this again and again for each heat and, finally, for the last three-lap dash to victory. (He almost always wins.)

The other racers take a dim view of Willy's antics, but the increasing crowds of fans love him.

ROAD RACING

Just as demanding, but in a different way, is bicycle racing on roads. Road racers are a slim, trim, rock-hard group who use a somewhat different, heavier bike with gear changes and front-

Road racing is a very demanding bicycle sport for experienced riders.

and rear-wheel brakes. They ride longer distances over streets and highways.

One recent road race in France was a distance of 750 miles, non-stop. Teams from all over the world arrived to compete in this race from Paris to Brest and back to Paris. Though the United

States racers were given little chance to do well in this favorite race of French cyclists, American Scott Dickson finished in second place out of 1800 entrants. Dickson beat many of the top European amateur cyclists and shook the European bicycle establishment. Normally they look at American riders with an unworried smile when it comes to road racing.

It is true that Americans generally do not even recognize the names of the top bicycle racers as they might the names of other athletes like A. J. Foyt, Kareem Abdul-Jabbar, or Steve Garvey. But John Howard, George Mount, Bruce Donaghy, and the brother combination of Dale and Wayne Stetina are remarkable athletes competing in a grueling sport. And there are others in bicycle racing, top stars who, with the rise in popularity of bike racing, might soon be very well known. Eventually America might be like Europe, where you can ask almost anybody and they will instantly know the names Bernard Hinault, Feliece Gimondi, or Eddy Merckx. Most European fans know as much about these racers as Americans know about their well-known athletes. For bicycle racing is an accepted major sport in most European countries.

How tough is road racing on a bicycle? This is the type of racing you can get hooked on if you try it, as tough as it is. It is challenging, demanding, even painful, but it tests your body and your bicycle to the limit, and when you complete a race you feel a surge of joy and accomplishment.

Here is an example of the qualification requirements for a race such as the Paris-Brest-Paris event. You qualify if you can cover the following distances in the times noted:

200 kilometers in 14 hours
300 kilometers in 20 hours
400 kilometers in 27 hours
600 kilometers in 40 hours

Most cyclists would be eliminated in early qualifications.
The Tour de France is another very popular European bicycle

race. Riders cover more than 2500 miles in about twenty-one days. The rider with the shortest total time wins.

This doesn't mean that you can't begin to road race by trying some of the shorter American races, or even the more informal races held by clubs throughout the country. One very popular American race is the Tour of Somerville, New Jersey, a fifty-mile road race.

There is no professional road racing in America but amateur racing, governed by the United States Cycling Federation, is booming. For the more formal amateur road races, where the experts compete, there is a series of qualification events called "criteriums." They are races around short courses—city blocks, as a general rule—to determine a racer's basic ability and seed

In 1886, this "racer" led the pack.

him or her into the major road races. Most races include dozens or even hundreds of racers and are often started in sections, with the slower riders leaving the line first, followed by the faster qualifiers.

There are checkpoints at intervals along road courses where riders get identification books stamped, to prove they actually did pass by. They can also replenish their water supply or grab a quick snack, then rejoin the pack. There is normally a difference of many hours between the first and last finishers in a long bicycle road race.

In the 1890's, the sport of bicycle racing was known as "the bloody sport" because of the many injuries to cyclists. Riders are still injured, primarily because if a bike begins to fall out of control, the rider must fall with it. Their feet are strapped to the pedals so they can't reach out with a leg and catch themselves.

One rider was warming up for the upcoming Los Angeles Classic, a part of the 1980 California Criterium Series. Meanwhile, officials were putting up the start/finish banner that stretched all the way across the street. A rope hanging down from one corner of the sign caught the rider as he streaked under and he crashed hard. Fortunately he was only stunned, but spectators once again saw the dangers, even the unexpected ones, of road racing.

Also popular in bicycle racing are track events like the *Miss and Out* race. Here, the last rider on each lap is eliminated. Only a few remaining riders (a number determined by the promoter) dash for the finish on the final lap. Then there is the *Points Race*, where riders must sprint for points on designated laps. The winner is decided by points.

In the *Handicap Race*, riders get head starts according to their skill and experience, or lack of them. In the *Motor Pace*, each rider is paced by a small motorcycle. The motorcycles offer wind protection as the riders get close behind and "draft" just like race cars. These bicycle racers reach much higher speeds than racers without pacers.

Racers are extremely competitive. This rider stopped in a short race to change a rear wheel, though he knew it would ruin his chance for victory. But in seconds he was back in the race.

If you are a new rider planning to train for long-distance racing, some experts insist that you should start with a lower pedal rpm even though a faster one might normally be more efficient. They say that it is inefficient for a beginner to go at 90 rpm. Try 60 rpm, since even road and track racers begin training every season at a lower rpm, then work up to the faster spin. As conditioning increases and endurance improves, they rebuild the rpm count.

While training, use toe clips. They are necessary for a smooth, consistent pedal cadence and to help with ankling. Then find an area where you can train steadily, without the need to constantly stop for traffic and traffic lights. Select a gear that will allow you to maintain a steady pedal cadence for an extended period of time, lowering the gear if the effort becomes difficult.

To get the rpm, count your pedal revolutions for six seconds, then multiply by ten. Try for 60 rpm by changing the gears. Concentrate on a smooth pedaling motion. You will feel the slightest changes in grade as you improve your rhythm, and as you do, concentrate on keeping the cadence steady by changing gears. You should always be applying the same pressure on the pedals and maintaining the same rpm, though the speed of the bike will vary with hills and grades.

Distance riding, believe it or not, will soon become as effortless as walking.

6
SAFETY

Safety is a dull subject. Who wants to be worrying about being safe during an activity as exciting as cycling? I'll tell you who. Me! And you, too, though it doesn't have to be a mind-filling problem that interferes with your fun.

The fact is, there are more and more bicycles being ridden on the streets and highways by more different kinds of people. More cyclists means more accidents, for that is a statistical certainty. The unfortunate truth, the same statistics show, is that in about eighty percent of bicycle/automobile accidents the biker was not obeying basic rules of the road.

On the other hand, cyclists have fallen into the same class as runners when it comes to antagonizing a certain breed of automobile drivers. Nobody has yet been able to explain why these dim-witted drivers are threatened by the presence of a bicycle, even if the cyclist is far to the side and in no way interfering with the progress of the car.

Perhaps it is because they feel guilty, sitting there in their soft seat while they use unrenewable fuels and pollute the air, all the time growing less and less fit. They know they are "using an atom bomb to kill a canary" for in most cases they are alone in their car, using a 5,000-pound machine to get one person a few miles down the road.

So these numskulls resent runners, cyclists, and others who believe in doing their own thing in their own way without bothering their neighbors. What do they do about it? The more bicycle

Always obey the rules of the road, as this cyclist is doing.

literature you read, the more frightened you can become. They swerve their cars in an intentional effort to "nick" a cyclist. Isn't that *fun*? They don't seem to want to *kill* you (thanks a lot!) but only to cause you to back off, or to take a spill. More professional truckers than you would ever believe—you know, the guys we always believed were the best drivers on the road—seem to get a kick out of brushing back cyclists with the huge mirrors jutting out from the sides of their monsters. With a hearty laugh and a great belch of fumes, these "good buddies" then roar on down the road while watching your distress.

Experienced cyclists have long since learned to beware of another danger on streets and highways. These are the teen-agers who have only recently been awarded the right to drive, and who must rush out and prove their right to the highway, *all* of the highway. Fortunately, most teen-agers have had driver's education courses and know enough to be careful. And of these others, most soon grow out of this phase but for a while they are real pistols. You must be especially careful of these menaces, and if they are on the road, especially if they are in a junior-sized pickup truck, stop, get far off the road, and cringe behind some nearby cover until they are at least a mile on down the highway.

You doubt all this? It gets worse. Most local law enforcement officers will do little to help you. You can be harassed, brushed back, even nicked, and they will grudgingly take a report on the matter. That's about it. Unless they see such an occurrence, or unless you are seriously injured, they are rather disinterested. You have a license number? Oh, OK, they'll write it down and "see what they can do" but don't expect much. You have witnesses? They'll shake their head, make more notes, and promise to look into the matter. But don't expect to see your antagonist in court.

It does happen, but rarely. Nor is this a matter of an accident, which also happens with alarming regularity. This is purposeful vehicular harassment and, occasionally, injury.

Accidents, pure and simple, happen all the time. One western rider of great experience had a rule. He never rode past the front of another vehicle unless he had solid eye contact with the driver. Eye contact. The two, the driver and the cyclist, are looking directly into each other's eyes so that no mistakes can possibly happen.

Recently he spent a week in a hospital after a driver pulled out of a driveway and ran over him. He saw the driver and the driver seemed, by eye contact, to see him. But the driver thought he was going to stop. Vehicular laws give the bicycle the same advantages as automobiles, but who is to know?

In another case a rider was sent sprawling into a ditch after getting knocked down by the right mirror of a semi-truck. The cyclist was over into the soft shoulder to allow the truck plenty of room, but the trucker wasn't about to change his own course for any two-wheeler. After all, they shouldn't be allowed on the highway, should they? So the mirror became a cow-catcher, which at least was better than getting hit by the truck itself.

And what about the long line of riders who were sent reeling in all directions by a carful of teen-agers coming from the other direction? The car crossed over into the oncoming lane and scattered them like a row of dominoes. Or the girl cyclist who only complained after a certain driver had passed her again and again while the passenger reached out and grabbed the most obvious part of her rearward anatomy. One time she could take, but several times repeated?

You might want to deal with such a situation more directly, should you see it happen. These teen-age bullies are difficult to catch because in spite of their bluster and bravado, they are cowards at heart. You'd probably enjoy beating them up, but they run very fast.

Why do drivers fail to see, or purposely harass, cyclists? The poor cyclist only wants to be left alone, but under the circumstances safety becomes very important. The more you ride, the more you realize this. On the day you see a bicycle rider attack a speeding car or truck, you can tear out this chapter and throw it away.

HOW TO RIDE IN TRAFFIC

Meanwhile, at least read through the following list of suggestions for your safety. Let's take the dozen basic rules of the road, adapted from those suggested by the Schwinn Bicycle Company, a firm that has every reason to hope that cyclists remain alive and healthy.

Be especially careful of car doors that might open in front of you.

1. Obey all applicable traffic regulations, signs, signals, and markings. Bicycles are subject to the same traffic laws as cars, wherever they apply. A good rule of thumb is to avoid congested streets and use bikeways, lanes, or paths where possible.

2. Obey all local ordinances pertaining to bicycles. If your city, county, or state requires registration, licensing, or inspection, comply. If they don't want you to ride on sidewalks, don't do it. It is your responsibility to know these laws. Most police officers do not really know the laws governing bicycles, so help them by

carrying along a copy of local ordinances. Then ride within these laws yourself.

3. Keep right; drive with the traffic, not against it. Ride in a single file if there are more than one of you. Keep as close to the curb as practical. If you are riding two abreast, a minor swerve could be very serious, forcing you into traffic.

4. Watch out for drain grates, soft shoulders, and other road surface hazards. Be careful of loose sand and gravel, especially at corners. Watch out for potholes. Experienced cyclists try to ride ahead of themselves.

5. Listen for cars coming up from the rear or for cars pulling out into the traffic lane. For some reason, drivers pay scant attention to cyclists coming from the rear.

6. Don't carry passengers or packages that interfere with your vision or control. A good rule is "one person, one bike," unless it is a tandem model. Use baskets or luggage carriers for packages.

7. Never hitch a ride on a truck or other vehicle. This is an idiotic invitation to disaster.

8. Be extremely careful at intersections, especially when making a left turn. Look everywhere, twice, then look again. Most accidents happen at intersections. If traffic is heavy, get off and walk your bike with the pedestrian traffic. Then if they insist on hitting you, you have them—or at least your next of kin has them.

9. Use hand signals to indicate turning or stopping. Let the motorists around you know exactly what you intend to do by giving the appropriate signals loud and clear.

10. Protect yourself at night with the required red reflectors and lights. State laws vary, but most require a headlight and tail-light or red rear reflector for night riding. Some states require reflective pedals, additional side reflectors and other devices, but why not use them all whether they are required or not? You need all the protection you can get.

11. Ride a safe bike. Have it inspected to keep it in good mechanical condition. Your bike should fit you and should have

all components—especially brakes, shifting mechanisms, sounding devices, tires, spokes, saddle, handlebars, and lights (and all nuts and bolts)—correctly installed, tightened, and in working order. Listen for any noise that might alert you to a mechanical problem.

12. Drive your bike defensively. Remember that you can see much better than the motorists around you. Observe the car in front of you and the one in front of him. Leave yourself plenty of room to take defensive action if necessary.

Here's one more, to make the list a "baker's dozen":

13. Avoid pedestrians, especially where local ordinances permit riding on sidewalks. Give walkers the right of way whenever possible and don't sneak up behind them. This could startle them into stepping into you.

What about wearing a helmet?

More and more cyclists are wearing helmets. Many would not ride to the corner store without first donning their lightweight but life-protecting "skid lid."

"To think that I actually considered not wearing a helmet for that short trip makes me shiver," said one cyclist in a recent magazine letter. "I urge all of my fellow bikers to please buy and use a helmet."

This biker had been hit by a car on a routine errand to the neighborhood store. The driver of the car ran a red light and hit him broadside at 40 mph. Though the cyclist was injured, the helmet saved his life.

The wearing of a helmet and other safety pads and extra reflectors are a matter for the cyclist to decide. Helmets are light and ventilated, but they are still another piece of gear you must wear. If you hit your head in a fall you will be glad you were wearing a helmet, or you will wish, if you are able to wish, that you had been wearing one. Many automobile drivers are killed each year because they didn't hook up their seat belts. Why didn't they? Maybe they were in too much of a hurry to get going, or it was inconvenient, or they took the risk because they'd gotten away with it so far.

The same is true with cyclists. Most experienced bikers own at least one helmet. The true "bikey" wears a helmet, yet seldom if ever falls. Of course all participants in bicycle sporting events wear helmets, which should tell you something about them.

You can get helmet information, including statistics on wear versus non-wear, from the following sources. You probably won't fall and hit your head, but . . .

Bell Helmets, Inc.
15301 Shoemaker Avenue
Norwalk, CA 90650

Pro-Tec, Inc.
11108 Northrup Way
Bellevue, WA 98004

Bikecology Bike Shops
P.O. Box 1880
Santa Monica, CA 90406

Schwinn Bicycle Company
1856 North Kostner Avenue
Chicago, IL 60639

Kucharik
17125 South Western Avenue
Gardena, CA 90247

Skid-Lid Manufacturing Company
650 4th Avenue
San Diego, CA 92101

Mountain Safety Research
631 South 96th Street
Seattle, WA 98108

PROTECTING YOUR BICYCLE

Bicycles are one of the items most likely to be stolen. Police impounding garages are full of bikes, sold at periodic auctions because nobody has any idea who the real owner is. If you lock your frame to a tree, they steal your wheels. If you lock the wheels to the frame, they steal the accessories.

You can fight back.

A lock or a chain merely slipped through the front wheel or front sprocket does not provide the protection you need. The proper way to lock your bicycle is to wrap the chain through the

Police impounding areas in every town are generally loaded with bicycles because nobody knows to whom they belong.

frame and around the rear wheel, then around a post or some other stationary object. Be sure the lock is fully closed.

On bikes equipped with quick-release hubs, take off the front wheel and lock it with the rear wheel and frame. Because thieves have been known to cut off wooden posts to get to a bicycle, lock your bike to concrete or metal objects.

There is a cartoon showing a man standing before the desk sergeant at a police station. He looks full of woe. Dragging behind him is a giant ship's anchor chain. One of the links has been cut. "Somebody stole my bike," he is lamenting.

Use a lock and chain of case-hardened steel. The lock should have a shackle with a diameter of not less than ⅜ inch. The worst economy of all is to buy an expensive bicycle, then to lock it with a cheap lock and chain. Plan to spend twenty-five dollars or so for a locking device. Some lock and chain manufacturers include a guarantee on their equipment. If your bike is stolen by a thief who cuts through their lock or chain, they will pay some or all of the cost of a replacement bike.

Contact the following companies for more information on bicycle locks:

Atlas Lock Company
9121 South Sepulveda
Los Angeles, CA 95045

Master Lock Company
Milwaukee, WI 53210

Bike Security Systems
177 Tosca Drive
Stoughton, MA 02072

Here's another list to struggle through, but once you've read it you'll have an idea of how to protect your bike from theft:

1. Lock your bike every single time you you leave it unattended. Don't make the mistake of leaving it unlocked and unattended for "just a minute."

2. Put your bicycle away in a locked room, shed, garage, or basement when you are not riding. Don't leave your bike in a yard or driveway where it can be seen. Many cyclists take their bikes into their home, office, or factory rather than locking them outside. Never leave your bike outside at night.

3. Record the serial number of your bike and keep the number in a safe place so you can identify the bike if it is stolen. Register the bike with the police if such a service is available in your area.

4. If you or your family have homeowner's or apartment dweller's insurance, check to see if the policy covers your bike. If not, have a rider to the policy added to cover the bike.

5. Engrave all removable parts of your bike with the serial number or your own social security number. The serial number is usually found in three places: on the head tube under the manufacturer's name or insignia, on the underside of the pedal crank housing, and on the left rear toe plate near the axle.

6. Place all locking devices, chains, cables and the like as high off the ground as possible. This makes it more difficult to smash

Register your bike with the police if you have that service in your town, and listen to a police officer when he talks to you about safety.

or pry, or to gain leverage by using the ground as a brace, to break the locks.

7. Keep your bike in a well-populated, well-lighted, conspicuous area.

8. Take a color photograph of your bike to help police identify it in case it is stolen.

WHAT YOU CAN DO

One of the major problems with bike riding is motorists. You can help to make them aware of you and your right to the road.

The vast majority of motorists are not teen-aged menaces but responsible drivers. The last thing they want is to harass you, or to have an accident with you. Many of them, though, do not know the rules. Many of them do not know that you have an equal right to the road, that you must obey the same laws and receive the same courtesies as any other vehicle.

Have you seen the little pamphlets sent out by the oil companies with their monthly bills? Suggest to them a flyer aimed at educating motorists about a cyclist's rights and responsibilities. After all, the oil companies are pressing us to conserve fuel. Who does that better than a bicyclist? The Bicycle Manufacturers Association says that if every automobile trip of two miles or less were made by a bicycle instead, there would be 2.5 *billion* gallons of gasoline saved in a year.

Most broadcasting companies must donate time for public service announcements. This is controlled by the Advertising Council, so a word to them might bring about some public service announcements on the bicycle's legitimacy and right to the road.

Put a bumper sticker on your family car advising other motorists to be aware of cyclists and their rights. Something like I SHARE THE ROAD WITH CYCLISTS can't hurt.

Promote the use of "talking" bikes, electronically wired bikes used by police departments in public school safety demonstrations. These bikes "talk" to the students, getting a safety message across in an entertaining way.

"Have you ever seen a bicycle that has been run over by an automobile?" one such bike asks with a catch in the voice. Then, after a pause, the bike answers glumly, "What a *sickening* sight!"

Use your own bicycle safely and intelligently. Create among others the idea of the safety, efficiency, and ecological logic of bicycling. Remember, it isn't necessary for you to be an adult to impress younger riders or adults. Age has little to do with intelligent cycling, or with the ability to reach others by setting a good example.

In Europe, where bicycling has always been popular, there are now safer road conditions thanks to separate bicycle lanes and bike traffic signals. To get this kind of protection from automobile traffic, bicyclists have formed organizations, held rallies, put pressure on government, fought for publicity, and taken other direct action.

Ask your local government body (city council, city manager, etc.) to form a Bicycle Technical Advisory Committee for your town. Such a committee of citizens can be a big help in getting bike lanes and promoting bike safety.

Can you handle one more quick list? The Schwinn Bicycle Company stresses a list of "Don'ts" that are worth looking over:

1. Don't jump curbs with your bicycle. Curbs, potholes, railroad tracks and other obstacles can cause damage to tires, tubes, rims, and the front fork. *Lift* yourself over such obstacles by rising from the saddle and helping your bike by raising the handlebars.

2. Don't ride double unless your bike is a tandem. Doubling up increases the chances of an accident, and besides that the extra weight is hard on your bike.

3. Don't stunt. Your bike was built to take certain stresses, probably not (unless it is a BMX model) dirt riding or other jumping. Welds can break, wheels can collapse, forks can bend, and other damage can result.

4. Don't drop your bicycle. Use the kickstand or carefully lean the bike on a solid object. There are devices such as the Rhode Gear "Flickstand" (Box 1087, Providence, RI 02901) that lock the front wheel to the frame and make the whole bike rigid. It won't roll when leaned, even with a heavy load of touring gear.

5. Don't modify your bike unless you know exactly what you are doing. Certain types of equipment such as the long, foolish-looking "chopper" forks and high saddle struts should not be installed under any conditions.

6. Don't allow your bike to remain dirty. Mud, grit, and grime

should be cleaned off as soon as possible after a bicycle has been exposed to poor weather conditions. The finish can be damaged otherwise, and so can bearings.

7. Don't allow nicks and scratches to remain on your bike. You get that type of damage by not using kickstands, by parking in crowded areas, by letting locks and chains bounce about, and by laying the bike on the ground. Keep the paint touched up and waxed, to prevent rust.

One of the most dangerous of all accidents usually results from the locking of the front wheel of a bicycle. Such an accident often results in injuries. Some cyclists have been paralyzed or even fatally injured from flying over the handlebars after a front wheel has locked up. There are certain precautions a cyclist can take to help prevent this disaster.

Be careful about bags and clothing that might get caught in the front wheel. If you hang a raincoat over the handlebars, it will find its way into the spokes. Such an accidental jamming might at least give you a moment of warning, since the wheel might turn a couple of more times before jamming, but the result can still be quite serious.

One young rider had a wrench taped to a carrier over the front wheel. The wrench vibrated loose, fell into the wheel, and jammed across the forks. He was flipped over the hood of a car.

Be very careful how you mount any equipment on or near the front wheel. One generator was shaken loose and jammed into the wheel, causing an instant locking. The rider suffered a concussion and facial injuries. Generators, in fact, should be mounted on the rear wheel but if the unit must be on the front wheel, be sure it is in a forward position where wheel rotation will carry it away from the fork rather than into it.

A caliper brake can become detached and lock the front wheel instantaneously. The front brake holding devices should be inspected before every ride and locking washers or nuts should always be used. Consider strapping the brake cable to the frame near the brake assembly so that if the assembly does come loose, it won't fall into the wheel.

One man bought two bikes from a department store and had them assembled by a local mechanic. On the very first ride, the man's wife was thrown over the handlebars when a fender came loose and jammed the front wheel. Facial injuries, lost teeth, and a broken jaw were the price she paid for one forgotten mounting nut securing the fender to the fork crown.

Even one of the most modern safety devices, spoke reflectors, can come loose and jam between the spokes and the fork. Be sure the reflectors are the correct size and type for your bike wheels and be sure they are mounted solidly.

One student was cycling along when she saw a pothole in the road. Correctly, she lifted up on the handlebars to lessen the shock —and the front wheel fell off. Serious injuries resulted. Every cyclist must be certain that the holding nuts on the front wheel are secure even though new bicycles now being made to conform to the Consumer Products Safety Commission's standards must incorporate a means to prevent this loss of the front wheel, even if the nuts come loose. Some experienced cyclists squeeze the front forks together so that they must be spread apart to install the wheel.

Any part of a bicycle can fail. The front fork or front wheel can collapse, resulting in a devastating accident. It is true that any part of *any* mechanical device can fail, a situation difficult to guard against. But being aware of the possibility of mechanical failure can make a cyclist tend to ride in a safer way. If you thought of a wheel as being able to fall out of the dropouts, you might lift the handlebars a little more gently under certain riding conditions.

According to the Health Insurance Association, riding bicycles is going to bring better health to millions of new riders, but a few of us are going to get injured, or worse. Cycling, according to many experts, is better for you than jogging and much less monotonous. You can keep in shape with three or four sessions per week, a half hour to an hour per session. At only five miles per hour, you are burning 4.5 calories per minute more than when you are sitting still.

But none of this matters if you are unsafe in your riding. A slim, trim, physically fit body can be injured almost as severely as one that is out of shape. Don't make safety a chore, but keep it always in mind as you ride. Give your bicycle a pre-ride check before *every* ride. This is a simple matter that becomes a pleasant routine after the first few times:

1. Look over your bike for any loose nuts, bolts, connections, or attachments.

2. Check the brakes, front and rear, to be certain they are functioning properly.

3. Be sure nothing has slipped out of adjustment since the last ride (seat, handlebars, etc.).

4. Be sure all warning devices are solidly mounted and working properly (lights, horn, reflectors, etc.).

5. Look at your tires to be sure inflation is correct, wear is even, and rubbing is not occurring.

Now if you still want to be a cyclist, read on to learn how much good the sport can do you.

7
PHYSICAL REASONS FOR CYCLING

Anna McVerry is a registered nurse working with a cycling doctor in California. She loves cycling.

"It makes me feel good. Bicycling gives my whole body a chance to be active," says nurse McVerry. She tours with her husband, a confirmed cyclist, and she uses her bicycle for local errand running. "There is a wonderful fitness benefit from cycling, and it is the type of sport you can do alone or with company.

"I ride alone and sometimes I ride with others. Cycling is also a cheap sport when you compare it to skiing and many of the other physical sports."

Anna McVerry is a medical expert who is sold on bicycling as a sport and as an efficient, healthful way to travel. She loves it.

Remember Dr. Paul Dudley White's discussion of bicycle riding in the first chapter of this book? This presidential physician felt that bicycling, more than any other sport, promoted cardiovascular fitness because of the necessary action of the legs.

Let's ride as the experts ride, for in these techniques you will find the greatest benefits in general health, endurance, and distance covered. A cyclist who has been riding for a while and has learned by experience will use only about *one-half* the energy a beginner does to cover the same distance. This means that the expert can cover twice the distance with the same amount of work. Would you like to learn to ride like that?

Then take it easy, very easy, to start with, and work up to it.

As you do so, learn the riding techniques and advantages your bike offers. Then use this information.

Did you know, for example, that an expert does not pedal his bike with his legs to make it go? The expert uses all the muscles in his body as a team. The legs and arms and back all work together and without strain to propel the bike. They share the load. By sitting correctly in the saddle and traveling at a smooth, even pace with a rhythmic pedal motion, you are requiring your body to do less moving and thus less work.

The expert often uses the drop-type handlebars to lower and further streamline the body, but this is not absolutely necessary. Tests have shown that the rider using the more upright, all-rounder bars is riding at eighty-nine percent of the efficiency of the drop-type bar user. So with the lowered body you are being about eleven percent more efficient. Many riders will sacrifice this for what they consider to be a more comfortable upright position during pleasure riding. Of course all expert competitive riders use the drop bars.

Experts don't just pedal down with each foot, alternately, and then allow the foot to ride back up for the next downstroke. They pedal *around*. (See "Ankling, Toe Clips, and Straps," page 52.) All of these techniques further develop leg muscles as well as riding endurance and distance.

The real sign of an experienced rider is the track left behind. If the line is perfectly straight without wavering, if the rider shifts gears without losing speed or veering from a straight line, if the rider uses his hands and feet in concert, using no motion but that necessary to get the job done, the result is beauty in cycling.

WHAT ABOUT DIRTY AIR?

You may be one of the lucky ones who ride in clear and clean air far from the smog and pollution of big cities. Good for you.

Many cyclists are not so lucky. They must consider the problem of breathing dirty air.

The hazard of cycling in polluted air is real. Bicyclists breathe deeply, so it is even worse than merely living or walking in dirty air. The built-in systems in our bodies that filter the air we breathe work less and less efficiently as we breathe faster and harder. Then, too, only the particulate pollutants are filtered out by the nose and the bronchial tube systems—the soot and dust and pollen and other bits and pieces floating around in the air. The gases are not filtered, and they can be a real problem.

This will come home to you the next time you are cycling your way through a traffic jam during the rush hour. By the time you get through, you might have a sinus headache, runny nose, watering eyes, a chronic cough, and you will probably also have a lowered resistance to respiratory infections.

Perhaps the greatest worry of many cyclists, carbon monoxide, should be lowered on the list of worries to rank below other gases such as sulfur and nitrogen oxides. These gases, when they come into contact with the damp surfaces of the lungs, can cause the formation of sulfuric and nitric acid. Meanwhile, carbon monoxide is being removed by natural means from the body almost as fast as it enters due to the rapid breathing of the cyclist. A recent study showed that the level of CO_2 in the body of cyclists was substantially less than that in motorists.

The solution, if you are a big city rider and have more concern for your health than for your appearance, could be the wearing of a respirator. More city cyclists than you might imagine are now doing just that. A respirator such as the Norton Model 7513 (The Norton Company, 2000 Plainfield Pike, Cranston, RI 02920) will allow you to ride through the heaviest traffic without worrying about pollution harming your lungs. The air you will be breathing will be almost as pure as fresh mountain air.

Simple maintenance, which includes cleaning the mask and filters, is necessary only at intervals. There is a side benefit from wearing the mask, too. Not only does it seem to frighten away strange dogs and potential harassers, but it also makes everybody, including motorists, aware of what is happening to the air we all must breathe.

The alternative, since breathing polluted air is known to be a hazard and cyclists breathe it deeply, is to avoid situations where you are cornered as if in a giant gas chamber. Ride to school or work earlier and leave earlier, if possible, and try to avoid the routes where automobile traffic is heavy.

Speaking of taking things into the body that could harm you, don't mention your bicycle to Monsieur Mangetout of France, also known as "Mr. Eat-All." Mangetout's performances include *eating a bicycle*. He cuts it down into bite-sized pieces and then swallows it. The whole bicycle. He says he prefers the chain for its taste, but he eats everything, including the frame. Then, for dessert, would you believe he eats a television set?

HOW ABOUT LOSING WEIGHT?

Every expert cyclist has a similar appearance. They are lean, wiry and healthy. They seem to be able to eat anything (not including bicycles), for they burn up so many calories at their sport. Does this mean that cycling is a weight-loss method?

Yes.

Everybody has heard the arguments. "Why should I exercise in an effort to sweat off a few ounces when one single glass of water, which I'll desperately need, will put it all back on again?" "Why should I run around the block several times to burn off what one snack will put right back on?"

Weight problems know no age limit. Children, teen-agers, and adults have weight problems. But often the real problem is that the body's appetite control has been disrupted. You eat more, so you want to eat more, so you eat more, so your body asks for more, so you eat more—and on and on. So you get overweight.

But what if you didn't *want* to eat more?

Any doctor will tell you that if you take in more calories than you burn off, you are going to gain weight by storing the extra calories in fat. If you burn more calories than you are taking in, your body will use up some of its stored fat to provide the calories to burn. And everybody knows that cycling is a fine way to burn off more calories in a pleasant, efficient way. Basically, bike riding burns off from about five hundred to eight hundred calories per hour. That is just general bike riding, not high-speed, long-distance, or hard-work riding. The faster you ride, the more calories you will burn. The harder you work, the more calories you will burn. But in cycling, the work is *fun*.

"It is a pleasure to ride a bicycle. The air is fresh and the scenery is beautiful," says Dr. Herbert C. Hamel, Jr., a confirmed cyclist.

Hamel, who is also a runner, considers both activities about equal in health benefits. "But cycling is so much more fun," he says, "and it is much less strenuous."

Dr. Hamel bicycles back and forth to his office, carrying a "beeper" and using phone booths to return emergency calls. He also bicycles on his afternoon off in the beautiful beach and mountain country of Southern California. "It is great for coronary arteries and it is a tranquilizer. You can be all upset and then go cycling and feel so much better."

Dr. Hamel is concerned, as a general practitioner, about the increase in smoking among young people, especially young women. "But you can't smoke while riding a bicycle," he points out, "and it is certainly good for weight control."

In *The Doctor's Quick Weight Loss Diet*, Dr. Irwin Stillman writes that "energetic" bicycling uses up as many calories per hour as swimming, and more than tennis and running. It is easy for any of us to fool ourselves on the subject of exercise and calorie use. But most cyclists know that bicycling is unique as an exercise. You can go from using zero energy (coasting down a hill) to maximum energy (sprinting as hard as you can). Here's a chart devised by *Bicycling* magazine to suggest how cycling compares to other activities:

Walking compares to *slow cycling*

Backpacking
or } compares to *bike touring*
Slow jogging

Running compares to *fast touring or racing*

Once you have started regular exercise such as bike riding, your metabolic balance will gradually be readjusted. Your appestat, the body's automatic appetite control mechanism, will take over and you will eat as much as you need, not as much as your over-weight condition tells your body it wants.

A 150-pound teen-ager will expend about ninety calories per mile while running. He (or she) will use up two thousand calories by running about twenty-two miles per week, a modest regime for experienced runners. On a bicycle he will do the same by riding at about twenty miles per hour for a little over three hours, and he'll probably enjoy it a lot more (and he won't be risking injury to feet and legs).

It becomes, then, a matter of numbers. You can leave it where it is, you can cut the calories you take in, and/or increase the distance. You can control exactly how much weight you lose, bearing in mind that calorie starvation can result in decreased performance, loss of muscle mass, and even nutritional deficiencies.

Eventually you will reach that slim, sleek balance that most cyclists exhibit. But at first your body might fight you. It doesn't want to lose the weight it has become used to packing on. Like a squirrel storing nuts for the winter, the body tries to store fat (calories) for a "rainy day." You must take charge of your body, but do it slowly and easily. Don't frighten your body into thinking you have been thrown into a concentration camp on bread and water. Take it easy.

Remember one other factor. Muscle is more dense than fat. You might be losing fat but gaining muscle, so the total weight remains the same. Doctors will agree, though, that muscle is much better than fat, and improvement will be your reward if you stay with it.

BICYCLING AND CHOLESTEROL

You probably know people who have been told to reduce their cholesterol levels. Cholesterol deposits build up inside the arteries, obstructing the flow of blood, and this can lead to a heart attack in later life. Since the condition starts when we are young and deposits actually begin to accumulate, early exercise will control and even reverse it.

You do not have to be fat and fifty to concern yourself with the matter of cholesterol buildup. In fact, if you become fat and fifty, it may already be too late. But if you are sixteen and sleek, there is no reason for you ever to become fat and out of shape. Bicycling is the perfect answer (along with comparable sports such as running, swimming, and other aerobic activities). Cycle away the cholesterol deposits. Don't allow them to accumulate.

A recent survey by the famous Framingham (Massachusetts) Heart Study group uncovered the fact that cyclists who average as little as twenty-five miles per week have more healthful cholesterol levels than people who do not exercise, so every little bit helps.

Here's a plan to follow:

1. Exercise regularly, preferably by cycling at a regular pace for a regular distance of more than twenty-five miles per week.

2. Maintain your ideal weight. If you are overweight, reduce

to this weight. Check with your doctor about controlling or reducing your weight by limiting your intake of sweet and fatty foods.

3. Do not smoke.

LIMBER UP BEFORE YOU RIDE

Every athlete knows that "warming up" is very important to performance. You will do better in a game if you warm up your body before the game starts. The same is true for any of us, in any physical activity. You may not be riding off on a half-century or a century, and you probably won't want to take twenty minutes to warm up before your ride to the store for a loaf of bread. But you can use the exercises shown here (based upon yoga) to limber your body, warm your muscles, and generally prepare yourself for a ride that will make any demand at all on your body.

Depending upon what you plan to do or how far or how fast you plan to ride, do as many of these movements as you wish. Do one of them, a few of them, or all of them. You will feel better and your body will respond more quickly to the task you are asking it to perform. Cyclists are no different from runners, swimmers, or any other athlete. Warm-ups are important for any endeavor that will require the body to work.

SCOTT H. OLNEY

The Backbend. Bend back and grasp the ankles. Arch the back and hang the head as shown, then hold for a few seconds while breathing freely.

Head Rotation. With the back and shoulders straight, relax the neck muscles and roll the head in a series of circles. Do it slowly and gently.

Head to Knee. Sit on the ground with back straight and leg extended. Exhale slowly as you . . .

. . . bend over to touch your head to your knee. Inhale as you rise back up.

Forward Bend. Stand straight and clasp your hands behind your back, then . . .

. . . bend slowly forward as far as is comfortable, relaxing as you stretch.

Toe (or Ground) Touch. Bend over and touch the hands to the toes, or the ground.

Back Arch. Raise your body off the ground on your hands and feet, but relax and do it slowly and carefully.

WHAT ABOUT HOT WEATHER?

Bicycling is an ideal warm weather activity. Remember the last time you saw runners training on a hot day? They were probably reduced to a stumbling gait, gasping for air, and soaked to the skin with perspiration. Cyclists, on the other hand, find that the wind-chill factor of the forward speed helps to keep them cooler. But this can fool you. Cyclists must develop the same careful drinking habits that runners learn. Moisture lost through perspiration must be replaced. The body's thirst mechanism is not highly sophisticated. It does not always work to tell you that your body needs water by causing you to be thirsty.

One cyclist enjoyed a long hot California ride without once feeling thirsty. Nor did she ever feel the moisture of sweat on her body because of the very dry air. Still, during the ride, she drank *quarts* of water. She drank the water because she knew that if she did not, her performance would be seriously impaired. Never once did her body tell her it was thirsty.

She was following the old adage "Drink before you get thirsty." If you drink from your water bottle or from supplies along the way whether you are thirsty or not, you will keep your body's supply of fluid at a healthy level. You will not unknowingly sweat away fluids until you are in trouble, until it is too late to replace them for that performance period. You don't have to force down large quantities of water. Just sip away as long as it continues to feel right to you. Don't bloat yourself with fluids, but if the day is warm and you are working, you will find that your body will take in an amazing amount.

The best medical advice is that salt, and especially salt pills,

SCOTT H. OLNEY

Body Hang. One of the best ways of all to stretch and relax the muscles is just to hang by your hands.

should be avoided. Along with alcohol, coffee, and diuretics, all of which trick your kidneys into dehydrating you, salt intake should be limited until after the ride. The same is true of sugar and sweet drinks. Avoid the so-called "athletic" drinks unless you are on a long rest stop, because your stomach needs a larger share of blood to absorb them and that amount of blood is not available during heavy exercise.

Heat stroke occurs when the body core temperature increases too much. This affects the body's thermostat, the hypothalamus, in the brain and it stops trying to cool the body down when it needs it the most. The overheated body actually stops sweating, the temperature of the core can rise to as much as 110°, and death can result.

The signs of approaching heat stroke are plain. The body feels superhot, the skin is hot and red, but you may feel chilled (like a flu chill, with the body shaking). The head might throb, the vision might fade and blur, the breathing might become erratic, and thinking fuzzy.

Any victim of heat stroke or impending heat stroke should be placed flat on the back with the legs elevated a foot or so higher than the head. The application of ice and fluids to the skin will help to bring the body temperature down. This must be done promptly to save the victim's life, but treatment should not be continued past the point of bringing the temperature back to normal.

Summon medical aid.

Heat exhaustion is less severe, a condition where the body has become dehydrated. If you sweat more than you take in, you will probably face some degree of heat exhaustion. You'll feel tired and listless. If you keep exercising without replacing the lost fluids, your blood pressure will drop because the volume of blood is lower. This can put you into shock and can cause heat stroke.

The best thing to do is drink plenty of fluids while cycling, especially on a hot day. This simple precaution—whether you are thirsty or not—will nip the problem in the bud. Pay attention to experienced cyclists in this regard. Seldom will you see them without their fluid bottle.

TRAINING FOR COMPETITION OR LONGER RIDES

As you grow in cycling, you might want to compete. You will almost certainly want to extend your distance with weekend or longer touring. Whether the ride is for a few miles or to the next state, there are a few things you can do to condition yourself.

1. Stress aerobic training. This is training "with oxygen," or at a level of activity for which enough oxygen is available without panting or puffing. The oxygen comes from the air you are breathing.

Such aerobic training should be on a daily basis or at least every other day, with at least one rest day per week. Such training sessions should be for a minimum of twenty minutes of riding on level, easy terrain. More is better, of course, just so you are not straining.

2. Intermix at least once each week some anaerobic ("without oxygen") training in the form of sprint riding. Sprints are shorter-distance but much higher-speed runs on a bicycle. This rapid riding will cause the body to demand more oxygen than is available and will increase the capacity of the lungs to provide, and the blood to accept, extra oxygen.

3. Eat a balanced and complete diet with emphasis on a higher carbohydrate and lower fat content for a maintenance of glycogen stores in the body.

4. Eat adequate protein and include plenty of fiber with a minimum of salt. Raw vegetables and whole grains are excellent.

5. Get adequate rest between sessions.

6. Use no tobacco or alcohol.

7. See that your weight stays within the recommended range for your age and physical limits.

In the near future, Phase III Vector bikes like this one may replace fuel-consuming vehicles for city transportation.

8
HERE TO STAY

Bicycles have bounced up and down on the scale of popularity, but a new era has arrived. During the 1970's Americans bought more bicycles than cars—one hundred and three million bikes to one hundred and two million cars. Bicycles are inexpensive, energy-efficient, and healthful to ride. Cars are increasingly expensive to own and to operate. Today, even car people are switching to bikes.

The French people have always been bicycle riders. Recently some French politicians proposed that the government give a free bicycle to any driver who voluntarily relinquishes his driver's license. They are also lobbying for a law that will give everyone over sixty-five a free bicycle. In the United States, more than 700,000 people now ride bikes to work every day.

What happens when there is a transit strike and public transportation comes to a halt? Out come even more bicycles. During New York City's transit strike of 1980, bicycles filled the streets as people journeyed to work and back. After the strike, the number of people bicycling to work on a permanent basis had doubled. The same thing has happened in other cities.

Without question, bicycles are here to stay. But not, perhaps, in their present form. Exciting things are happening in bicycle design. Now being track-tested are experimental models that might become standard tomorrow. They are enclosed, high-speed bicycles with plastic canopies and much higher gear ratios. Although not yet ready for most riders, they offer both comfort and streamlined aerodynamic bodies. These are the Phase III bikes of the future. (Those we are now riding are Phase II, and Phase I bicycles were the contraptions first invented.)

Not that far into the future, it is quite likely that the average commuter will head for his garage a few minutes earlier in the morning. Not the commuter who must pedal only a mile or so to work. Many of them do that now. This is the commuter who must travel miles, from suburb to downtown, in all types of weather.

In the garage he will lift the sleek plastic canopy of his high-speed Phase III bike. Storing his tools and lunch box or brief-case in a compartment, he will lower the canopy, lean back in foam-padded comfort, fit his feet into pedal stirrups, and head for the street.

New gear mechanisms and larger gear sprockets will make pedaling much easier. Automatic gear shifters will select the proper sprocket combination according to road conditions and speed. Better designs and lubricants will cut friction in working parts.

This commuter will not be alone. All around in the new, heavily used bike lanes will be men and women in other models of Phase III bikes. Some will be fully enclosed, some partially enclosed, some elaborate and some less fancy. Many new manufacturers are already working on test models of such bicycles.

Most will have either a third wheel or two small helper wheels (like training wheels), so the bike won't tip over when stopped. All will have speedometers and other computerized gauges. Most will have roll bars in case the bike is bumped by one of the few automobiles still using the streets (restricted, of course, to special "auto" lanes for the safety of cyclists).

It will take a little longer, perhaps, to get to work, but it will be a healthful drive. The air will be cleaner. Hearts will be stronger and muscles in better tone. Given the opportunity to drive a car, most will still choose the sleek, efficient Phase III bicycle.

Why? Because they will have become so very logical. They will need not a cupful of precious gasoline or oil, nor a watt of electricity.

With streamlined protective sheathing, the new gearing, the extra space for passengers, high-torque drive systems, and interior heating against cold where necessary, they will be the best cost-effective transportation method of all. Nor will they be a slow or plodding means of getting where you are going. It could be that you will be able to *beat* the old "traffic jam" time. Especially when you consider what they are doing even today with Phase III bikes. A Phase III single-seat Vector bicycle currently being tested recently set a world speed record of 62.93 miles per hour.

Watch for these Phase III bikes. They'll be on the streets and highways sooner than you think.

Even sooner, a new, sleeker model of today's bicycle will be available. This model, resembling current Phase II bikes, will have a longer, lower frame for more comfort, a seat lower in the assembly, a new type of pedals, and cables and wires inside the tubing. There will be a new aerodynamically designed spoke pattern and large, two-inch foam-core tires. Fenders will make a big comeback as bikes return to being comfortable vehicles.

Phase II½ is just around the corner. Phase III will be here by 1990, and by 2020, according to some experts, human-powered vehicles will have almost completely replaced fuel-consuming vehicles as the primary means of city transportation.

That is in your lifetime.

9
MAINTENANCE

Although it doesn't overcome the major advantage of buying your bike from a recognized bike store, the purchase of a bicycle from a department store does offer one thing (besides a lower price). Some might not consider it much of an advantage, but you will have to put the bike together when you get it home. Whether or not you put it together right is another matter, for the assembly of a bike requires a knowledge of bikes and certain tools not usually available in the home shop.

At a bike store, they will do it for you. The bike came in the same box to them as it will to you, but they know exactly what to do with the frame, the wheels, the derailleurs, and the inevitable large plastic bag of little parts. They know what comes first, what comes next, and by the time they are finished with the bike it will be ready to ride away. It will be properly adjusted and lubricated and fitted to you.

Still, assembling a bike might at least teach you something, if only where to look when something doesn't work as it is supposed to work. The experienced cyclist knows his or her bike, and most cyclists quickly learn bike maintenance if not bike construction.

At a recent Los Angeles Grand Prime bicycle race, during the expert event, one cyclist struggled into the pit section near the starting line. Since the race was a criterium of only thirty-odd miles, a pit stop meant almost certain defeat. Still, these riders are intent upon winning and will try anything to keep going.

This rider had a soft tire. He couldn't possibly finish without a change.

In seconds he had stopped, loosened the back wheel, whipped off the chain and removed the wheel and gear assembly. At the same time he was shouting at a nearby friend, asking for the loan of his rear wheel. The friend, recognizing the problem, was at the same moment removing his own wheel. The exchange was made and the rider was quickly pedaling off in pursuit of the field. The pack had not yet appeared around the corner of the course, which was only two city blocks around. The rider was behind, but he was still on the same lap.

He *knew* his bicycle.

GUARANTEES

Many bicycle companies offer solid guarantees with their products. Schwinn Bicycle Company, for example, offers a *lifetime* guarantee. The bicycle is guaranteed, very simply, forever. If anything breaks due to any manufacturing defect or mistake, that part is replaced, or the entire bike is replaced. Perhaps that's why you see so many Schwinns on the streets after years of use. Other bicycle companies offer similar guarantees.

In fairness to Montgomery Ward, Sears Roebuck, J. C. Penney, and dozens of auto stores and other department stores who sell bikes, it must be said that they sell them cheaper. But they cannot afford to offer such sweeping guarantees. For one thing, they don't build their own bikes. The bikes are built by some other company, foreign or domestic, and sold under the logo of the retailer.

So if a frame breaks on a top-name-brand bike and you return the bike to the store, it will be repaired or replaced, free of charge. If it has broken because of a manufacturing defect, that is. Nobody guarantees bikes that have been run into a wall. If the frame of a department-store bike breaks (after any guarantee period), you will have to pay for a new frame.

Remember, too, that in this day of a boom in bicycles, department stores are jumping on the bandwagon. Their clerks may not understand bikes, but then neither do most of their customers as a general rule. On the other hand, bicycle specialty stores are always in the business of selling bikes. Their floor people are trained to know the product. They can help you, instruct you, fit the bike to you, and watch over it while you break it in. Most of them will ask you to bring the bike back after a period of time for a checkup, just to be sure every adjustment is still correct and everything is wearing in smoothly. The bike is not a toy to them, but a vehicle.

And the department store has probably charged you for assembly if you have allowed them to send it to their service department, thus bringing the price ever closer to the name brand model.

In any case, heavy maintenance should always be left to the experts. Whether you bought your bike at a bike store or a department store, the tough stuff should be done by a bike mechanic. If you break a frame, smash a wheel, bend a fork, or do some other drastic damage to your bike, take it to the bike store for repair. They'll do it better, quicker, and for not that much more money than you might have to pay somebody else with less experience.

Damages such as these often come from a collision with a hard object or some other major disaster. Many bikes—most bikes —never suffer such a collision (unless your bicycle gets run over by a car because you've carelessly left it in a driveway). You, yourself, will probably never have a serious accident on your bike. But if you do, it's nice to know there are experts around.

Meanwhile, somebody must routinely maintain the bike since it will probably never be in a shop. That is where you come in. Most cyclists take care of these chores themselves. Your bicycle will stay like new and you'll probably enjoy the tasks, for maintaining a modern bicycle properly is a pleasant challenge.

A BASIC TOOL KIT FOR BICYCLES

1. A 6-inch crescent wrench
2. A small-blade screwdriver
3. A pair of side-cutting pliers
4. A tire pump
5. A chain rivet extractor
6. A spoke wrench
7. A universal bicycle wrench
8. A can of WD 40 or similar penetrant
9. A small can of oil

Here are the parts of your bike that might normally fail or come out of adjustment, and the steps you should take to remedy the problem.

THE HEADSET

Sooner or later the fork of your bike might begin to feel loose in relation to the frame. Headsets do not stay in perfect adjustment forever. It is possible for a headset to seem to be too tight as well. Here is how to tighten one if it is loose, or loosen it if it is tight.

TO TIGHTEN

1. Loosen the locknut at the very top of the unit.
2. Tighten the threaded top bearing race with your hand if the surface is knurled, or with a large wrench (very gently) if the surface has flat areas like a nut. You should tighten down just enough to remove the looseness in the fork, but no more. It is better to tighten, test, then have to tighten a little more, than to get it too tight and score some bearings or races the first ride.
3. Retighten the top locknut.

1. If your front fork seems too tight, the problem is more than likely a dirty, dry headset that is binding up. The whole unit will need cleaning and relubrication, an interesting job if you take your time and be sure to get all the parts back together in the correct order. If dirt is not the problem, it is a simple matter to loosen the top locknut, then loosen the knurled top bearing race, then retighten the top locknut (just the opposite of the tightening steps).

2. To clean and lube, the parts will probably be, from the top, the locknut, a washer, the top knurled race, the top bearing, the top set race, then the head tube with the fork tube passing through to the bottom set of bearing and races. The bottom set, going on down in order, will probably be the bottom set race, the bottom bearing, and the fork crown race. Everything is tightened down from the top, where it is easy to reach.

3. Tap out the top and bottom set races, which are pressed into the head tube. As you loosen them, everything else will probably fall out. Have a place to keep all the parts and remember their order.

4. Inspect the bearings for wear and the races for damage or scoring, primary reasons for the tightening or binding of a headset. If everything looks good to you, clean all the parts in a solvent, then lightly grease them with a good bearing grease.

5. Reinstall the parts, making certain that the bearing races are even and flush against the edges of the head tube, then tighten the whole assembly with the knurled (or nut-shaped) top bearing race. Lock it all with the top locknut. Hand-tighten as snugly as possible without binding; if you must use a wrench, be very gentle.

THE CHAIN

The hardest-working, dirtiest part of your bicycle is the chain. The bike will operate with any number of problems, but it will not operate without the chain. The chain is the connecting link between your muscles driving the pedals and the rear wheel. Preventive maintenance of this part is absolutely necessary, and should be done frequently.

Chains stretch, and chains get dirty and rusty, with grit embedded in their links, all hastening wear.

DIRTY CHAIN

1. First try cleaning the chain by merely soaking a rag in solvent, then holding the rag around the chain as you turn the pedals. On all but coaster-brake models, turn the chain in reverse to clean it. On coaster-brake models, turn it forward after you have lifted the rear wheel off the ground.

2. If the chain is *filthy*, remove it from the bicycle by removing the rear wheel, then soak it in a solvent bath. Swish it around, bending it repeatedly so the solvent can work its way in between the rollers and plates of each link.

OILING THE CHAIN

1. What you want to do is get a *thin* coat of oil between the plates and rollers, with as little oil as possible anywhere else. Remember that oil attracts grime and grit, the very things you are trying to remove.

2. The best way is to remount the clean chain, then drip oil drop by drop onto the chain plates while the chain is being turned by the pedals. Do the dripping at the front chain sprocket and move the chain in reverse, if possible. Go easy with the oil. Less is more in this case. Finally, run the chain through a clean cloth to soak up any oil on the surfaces of the chain. You can get chain oil from your bicycle shop, but in an emergency any good household oil will do the job.

LOOSE CHAIN

1. On single-speed coaster-brake models and three-speed bikes you can tighten the chain by moving the rear wheel backward in

the dropouts. Loosen the nuts, move the wheel back, then re-tighten the wheel nuts. The chain should have about a half-inch of flex at the center, between the sprockets. Be sure to tighten the right rear wheel nut first, then align the wheel so that nothing is rubbing and the wheel is evenly between the rear chain stays. Finally, tighten the left rear wheel nut. You might have to loosen the coaster brake arm before moving the rear wheel on single- and three-speed bikes.

2. On ten-speed bikes, the tension of the chain is regulated by the derailleur. With all other adjustments correct, you might have to remove a link to tighten the chain, then modify the other adjustments. A small chain tool is needed for this job, since rivets must be driven out to remove a link. If you don't have the tool for this rarely needed job, take the bike to a bike store. It won't cost much at all, and they'll go over the other adjustments as well.

NOISY CHAIN

1. Sometimes one or more links bind up and cause a thumping or clicking noise as the chain passes over the teeth in the front sprocket or the rear sprocket assembly. Some dirt might have worked in between the rollers and the link plates. Maybe it is just a matter of a lack of lubrication. First, put a drop of oil on the offending link and try to work out the tightness. You might even try to loosen the link by very carefully using the blade of a small screwdriver between the rollers and the plates. But if the link is worn or bent, replace it.

REGULAR CHAIN MAINTENANCE

1. Once each week spray your bicycle chain with a cleaner such as Schwinn's DG-15 degreaser. Wipe it clean, then spray it with a good lubricant or drip oil on it as previously described. Be sure to wipe the chain after spraying or oiling. A toothbrush and a clean cloth come in handy whenever chain work is being done.

DERAILLEURS

Modern derailleurs will need attention periodically.

GENERAL LUBRICATION

1. Wipe off any accumulated dirt or grime from the derailleur with a clean rag. Then put one drop of oil on the pivot bolts. Use the oil very sparingly, since excess oil will only attract more grime. Wipe off any excess.

DERAILLEUR ADJUSTMENTS

1. If the chain is shifting by itself to a smaller sprocket, tighten the tension-adjusting screw on the shifting lever very slightly. Do not tighten too much or shifting will become very difficult.

2. If the chain will not shift onto the large rear sprocket, shift the chain to the smallest sprocket, then turn the adjusting barrel out of its holder until the cable is almost taut. (See Front Derailleur adjustment below.)

3. If the adjusting barrel on the rear derailleur is already unscrewed from its holder as far as possible, turn the adjusting barrel back into its holder and perform the following steps:

- Make sure the chain is on the smallest sprocket.
- Loosen the cable anchor bolt until the cable is free.
- Pull the cable taut with a pair of pliers.
- Hold the cable taut with the pliers and full-tighten the cable anchor bolt.

FRONT DERAILLEUR

1. The front derailleur is adjusted by limiting or extending the distance the derailleur cage will move. This movement is regulated by the high and low gear adjusting screws. These should be set to allow for the chain to shift onto each sprocket without going beyond and falling off.

141

CALIPER BRAKES

Lightly oil the caliper brakes between the arms of the pivot bolt as a regular maintenance chore. Do not use too much oil, whether your unit is a center-pull or a side-pull type. Both systems offer a positive means of braking the bicycle if the lever controls are applied with a firm, even pressure. A rule: Do not apply only the front brake—an especially important rule when you are riding on slippery streets, over gravel roads, or when turning.

POOR BRAKING

1. This condition may be caused by wheel rims that have become dirty, waxed, or oiled. The rim must be clean for caliper brakes to function properly. Use a clean cloth to wipe off any such deposits, including any wax from your last cleaning and waxing job or lubrication from oiling your chain or derailleur.

2. Poor braking may also be caused by the normal stretching of the brake cables or the wearing down of brake pads. A stretched cable or a partially worn pad can be corrected by turning the adjusting barrel above the brake levers or above the caliper until the brake shoes are approximately ¼ inch away from the wheel rim.

3. On a side-pull caliper brake, if the adjusting barrel is already unscrewed all the way before attempting adjustment, turn the adjusting barrel all the way back into its holder. Then loosen the nut on the cable anchor bolt. Hold the brake shoes about ⅛ inch from the wheel rim, pull the cable through the anchor bolt and hold taut, then tighten the nut on the anchor bolt and adjusting barrel. This technique may be used until the lugs on the brake pads are worn down, then you should replace the pads.

4. Another possible cause of poor braking might be that the cables need lubrication. This operation requires that the cables be removed from their housings, a job you might want to leave to the bike store mechanic.

SQUEALING BRAKES

1. Very gently twist the brake arms with an adjustable wrench so that the *front* part of the brake pad touches the rim *first*.

ONE SHOE TOUCHES THE RIM BEFORE THE OTHER

1. This condition can occur more with side-pull caliper brakes, and requires a gentle touch to correct. Loosen the mounting nut on the rear of the brake assembly until the entire caliper assembly is loose and can be rotated. Position the shoes in a manner that *overcorrects* the problem, then tighten as you hold the assembly in this position. Be sure you leave no mounting bolts and nuts loose.

BRAKE SHOES DO NOT RETRACT

1. This is often a matter of dry or rusty brake cables inside their housing, though you might try slightly loosening the mounting nuts and bolts on the caliper-brake assembly to see if that helps. Something could be binding. Otherwise, take the bike to a bike shop mechanic for lubrication of the cables.

WHEEL RIM

1. The wheel rims must be kept clean and unwaxed for caliper brakes to work efficiently. Be especially careful that lubrication from other assemblies does not get smeared on the wheel rims.

SPOKE ADJUSTMENT

The spokes are the wires that go between the wheel rim and the hub. They hold the wheel round, and though individually they may be springy and weak-appearing, they are quite strong when installed and adjusted. But they can be bent or broken, or twisted out of shape if you ride around running into hard things like curbs.

143

The spokes are held in holes in flanges on each side of the hub. At the wheel rim end they are screwed into nipples in holes. There are steel spokes, piano-wire spokes, stainless steel spokes, chrome spokes, and even shaped spokes, thicker at the ends and thinner in the middle where strength is not quite as important.

A general rule: All spokes on the same wheel should be the same type, size, and style. If you must replace a spoke, replace it with an exact copy of the one you are removing.

WHEEL WOBBLE

1. Bent or misadjusted spokes can pull a wheel out of round and cause it to wobble. The trouble is, you can adjust out one big wobble and create four little ones. Spoke adjustment is a tricky process, often left to a bike store mechanic who has the proper jigs and tools. Sometimes you remove a wobble from one side of the wheel only to create one on the opposite side.

2. If you are loaded with patience, give it a try. You can always take the wheel in to a mechanic if you make it worse. The brake pads make a handy point of reference if they are adjusted to the point where they barely brush the rim on each side. This will tell you exactly where the problem is as the wheel turns. You could even loosen the wheel and "cock" it in its dropouts until one side barely brushes the fork or frame. Try to think of the wobble as a group of errant spokes rather than just one. Is that group of spokes looser, tighter, bent, or what?

3. If you want the wheel rim to move left, tighten the spokes that go to the left side of the hub and loosen the spokes that go to the right side of the hub. Tighten and loosen a little at a time, checking the wobble constantly by spinning the wheel and watching your reference point. Work with a group of eight to ten spokes rather than one single spoke. Make greater changes in the center of the group and smaller changes out to the edges of the group. Each spoke should have the same tension (though this might not actually be the case). You can count the threads

showing on each spoke to check the tension. Keep working and you'll either get it right or run out of patience.

TIRES

There is a new tire that can't go flat or blow out. It features a thick, webbed inner construction and is made of long-lasting polyurethane that won't crack or rot. The Zeus Airless Tire (Zeus Manufacturing, Inc., P.O. Box 16397, Irvine, CA 92713) is doing well on the market. So is the No-Morflats (2075 South Valentia Street, Denver, CO 80231) tire.

For a softer, more traditional ride, most cyclists still prefer the old-faithful air-filled tire. But a number of things can cause tire failure in these tires:

>*Rupture:* caused by running over sharp objects.
>*Rim Bruise:* caused by running over curbs, potholes, etc.
>*Rim Cuts:* caused by rusty rims, overloading, etc.
>*Chafing:* caused by crooked wheels rubbing, etc.
>*Broken Beads:* caused by improper use of tools.
>*Sidewall Cuts:* caused by running over sharp objects.
>*Star Breaks:* caused by running over sharp rocks, etc.
>*Uneven Tread Wear:* caused by crooked wheels, skids, etc.
>*Blowouts:* caused by over-inflation, poor seating on the rim, etc.

Here's a tire-saving tip: If you are going to store your bicycle for long periods of time (over winter, for example) be sure to hang it up or turn it upside down. Tire casings can be distorted by the weight of the bicycle over a period of time.

TIRE REPAIR

1. Remove the wheel with the flat tire from the bicycle.

2. Completely deflate the tire, then remove the tire from the rim, using only your hands, on one side. Bicycle tires and tubes can be damaged by using metal tools, especially sharp tools like

screwdrivers, so be very careful if you *must* pop a bead loose with a tool.

3. Remove the tube and repair the puncture with a good patching kit, following the directions on the kit.

4. Examine the tire carefully. Examine the rim. Make sure the tire is clean and the rim free from rust and loose or rough spoke heads.

5. Make sure the rubber rim strip covers all the spoke heads.

6. Inflate the tube until it just starts to regain its shape, then put it back into the tire.

7. Insert the valve through the hole in the rim if you have taken it out of the hole, then carefully remount the tire on the rim using your hands.

8. Inflate the tire carefully until the beads are seated. Check to be sure that the beads rest properly in both sides of the rim and that the rim line on the tire is visible all the way around on both sides. Deflate the tube, allowing the tube to free itself. This avoids pinching and binding of the tube inside the tire.

9. Inflate the tube once again, this time to the correct pressure.

10. Replace the wheel in the frame of the bicycle.

ROLLING RESISTANCE

The amount of forward energy you generate is affected by the rolling resistance. Rolling resistance is made up of a number of factors, some of which you can control. More weight, for example, means more rolling resistance. The weight of your bicycle and, indeed, your own weight, are either here to stay or can be changed by the purchase of a new bicycle or a diet. Hub bearing friction can be reduced by proper hub lubrication and maintenance. Wind resistance on both rider and bicycle is something you must learn to live with, at least during one way of your round trip.

A large factor in rolling resistance is the flexing of the tires and the wheels as they roll. The flattening of the tire as it contacts the ground and its return to its normal shape as it moves on around take energy. A wheel without the proper tension will flex (as it should to some degree) and cost in energy.

Regular maintenance of tires and wheels, stressing tire inflation and spoke tension, will help keep energy loss to a minimum, thus reducing rolling resistance to a minimum. The trick with the newer, high-pressure tires is to keep the *footprint*, that part of the tire that meets the ground, as small as possible. Don't allow your tires to lose air, for this will enlarge the footprint and increase the rolling resistance.

Keeping your bicycle in good shape can be fun. It will certainly save money in the long run. For extended bicycle life, safer riding and more troublefree fun, follow this schedule.

A SIMPLE MAINTENANCE SCHEDULE

1. Adjust every month:
    - Side play in front and rear brake levers
    - Brake blocks and pads to wheel rim
    - Chain
2. Lubricate every month:
    - All levers (oil)
    - Head races and crown races (grease)
    - Brake joints (oil)
    - Wheel hubs, front, rear, and freewheel (oil)
    - Coaster and three-speed hub (1 tablespoon oil)
    - Chain (chain lube)
    - Bottom bracket (grease)
    - Pedals (grease)
3. Adjust and lube when required:
    - Reflectors and headlights
    - Tire pressure
    - Headset bearings (grease)
    - Wheel alignment
    - Handlebar

- Front and rear hub cones (oil)
- Pedal cone and bearings (grease)
- Front and rear derailleur (oil)
- Three-speed hub indicator (oil)

4. General Maintenance:
   - Polish enamel surfaces with a good liquid wax.
   - Use touch-up paint when needed.
   - Wax chrome surfaces, coat with oil in extremely wet conditions.
   - Clean tires.
   - Clean leather or plastic saddles.

SUGGESTED READING

BICYCLE MAGAZINES AND NEWSPAPERS

MAGAZINES

Bicycle Motocross Action
612 Meyer Lane, #9
Redondo Beach, CA 90278

Bicycling
33 East Minor Street
Emmaus, PA 18049

Bike World
Box 366
Mountain View, CA 94040

BMX Plus!
2458 West Lomita
Suite 217–219
Lomita, CA 90717

California Balloon Bike & Whizzer News
P.O. Box 765
Huntington Beach, CA 92648

League of American Wheelmen Bulletin
8053 Sykes Road
Richmond, VA 23235

Minicycle/BMX Action
7950 Deering Avenue
Canoga Park, CA 91304

ABA Action
P.O. Box 718
Chandler, AZ 85224

Bicycles Today
American Promotions, Inc.
1102 N.E. 4th Avenue
Ft. Lauderdale, FL 33304

NBA World
P.O. Box 411
Newhall, CA 91322

Velo-News (Bicycle Racing)
Box 1257
Brattleboro, VT 05301

GLOSSARY

adjusting barrel: A section of a cable mechanism where two parts thread together, making a length adjustment possible.

ankling: A pedaling technique to apply pressure on the upstroke as well as the downstroke by bending the ankles.

bead: The reinforced area around a tire where it is pressed against the wheel.

bearing:

  crank: The support unit between the crank axle and the frame that allows the pedals to turn with as little friction as possible.

  head: The support unit inside the head tube that allows the front wheel to be turned by the handlebars with as little friction as possible.

  wheel: The support units between the wheel and the axle that allow the wheel to turn freely and with as little friction as possible.

binding: Rubbing tighter and tighter against another part until no more motion is possible; freezing up.

blowout: Immediate and forced expulsion of air from a tire or tube through an opening caused by damage or failure.

brake blocks: That part of the caliper brake system upon which the brake pads are attached. The block is adjustable so that the pad fits exactly against the wheel rim.

brake pad: The rubber or composition part of the brake system, attached to the brake block, that rubs against the wheel rim, slowing the bicycle.

caliper brake: A unit that squeezes pads against wheel rims when a lever is operated, stopping the wheel.

chain: A flexible linked unit that passes muscle power from the chain sprocket to a sprocket attached to the rear wheel.

cleats, shoe: Projections on riding shoes used with rattrap pedals to enable the rider to power the bike on the pedal upstroke. (See *rattrap pedals.*)

coaster brake: A single-speed rear wheel hub unit with the brake components mounted inside. Pedaling in reverse applies the brakes.

conditioning: Getting the body, especially certain muscles, in shape for riding.

cone: A cone-shaped nut that holds ball bearings in place.

contour map: (See *topographical map.*)

cycling cape: A lightweight, waterproof cape for rainy weather allowing free body movement.

derailleur: The unit that shifts the chain from one sprocket to another. It is controlled by a lever and cable and operated by hand.

dropout: The slot in the front and rear frame where the wheel axles are mounted.

freewheel: A clutch in the hub of the rear wheel that allows it to run on free from the rear sprocket, as in coasting; also, the rear sprocket cluster of one to five (or more) cogwheels.

gears: Transmission mechanism that enables a rider to pedal more efficiently. Also referred to in bicycling as "speeds."

generator: A unit turned by the bicycle wheel to produce electricity for lights.

headset: The system of bearings and races mounted inside the head tube. (See *bearing, head.*)

hub cone: The bearing race in a bicycle wheel.

kickstand: A foldout stand to support the bicycle when it is parked.

locknut: A nut that is screwed down upon another nut to lock the first into position.

lug: A form-fitting sleeve welded or brazed in place where two sections of a more expensive bicycle frame come together.

lug weld: The weld or braze that holds the lug in place.

panniers: Saddlebags hung one on each side over the rear wheel of a bicycle.

race: The groove or channel in which roller bearings move.

rattrap pedals: Pedals with a cage around them, used on a bike ridden by a rider with cleated shoes. (See *cleats, shoe.*)

saddle: The seat of a bicycle.

score: A deep scratch or gouge in metal.

speeds: (See *gears.*)

spoke reflector: A reflector made to be mounted on the wheel spokes.

stem: The unit mounted into the headset to support the handlebar.

stunting: Doing "wheelies" or other riding tricks; should be done only under very controlled, safe conditions.

tandem bicycle: A bicycle built for two or more, with a seat, handlebars, and pedals for each rider.

three-speed hub: A rear-wheel hub with internal mechanism, controlled by a lever or a twist grip, to change the gearing of a bicycle.

topographical map: Also known as a contour map, showing details of the *shape* of the land, with mountain heights and valleys indicated.

tubular tires: Lightweight, one-piece, rather fragile tires generally used on racing bicycles.

wheelie: A stunt performed by lifting the front wheel of a bicycle and riding on the rear wheel only.

INDEX

CHAPTER 2